Access to English As a Second Language

1

Access to English As a Second Language 1

Robert G. Breckenridge
Alemany Adult School
San Francisco, California

McGRAW-HILL INTERNATIONAL BOOK COMPANY
New York   St. Louis   San Francisco
Düsseldorf   Johannesburg   Kuala Lumpur   London   Mexico
Montreal   New Delhi   Panama
Rio de Janeiro   Singapore   Sydney   Toronto

ACCESS TO ENGLISH AS A SECOND LANGUAGE, BOOK I

Library of Congress Cataloging in Publication Data

Breckenridge, Robert G
    Access to English as a second language.
    1. English language—Text-books for foreigners.
I. Title.
PE1128.B67   428'.6'4   72-8833
ISBN 0-07-007395-3

CONTENTS

Access to English As a Second Language 1

Lesson One

LISTENING DRILL

Step 1. Listen to your teacher pronounce the words below several times.
Step 2. Listen to your teacher say each word and decide if it is number 1 or number 2.
Step 3. Answer with the number when the teacher pronounces the words.

1	2
eat	it

READING

Centerville is a town in the United States. It is a large town. It has a lot of buildings. One building is a bank. Another is a store. Another is a supermarket. Another is a garage. One large building is a school. One small building is a house. It is the Bakers' house. You are going to learn a lot about the Baker family in this book. You are going to read about the Bakers and about Centerville, too.

"YES OR NO" QUESTIONS

Give the correct answer, "Yes, it is" or "No, it isn't."

1. Is Centerville a town? Yes, it is.
2. Is Centerville in the United States? Yes, it is.
3. Is Centerville in Mexico? No, it isn't.
4. Is there a school in Centerville?
5. Is there a bank in Centerville?
6. Do the Bakers live in Centerville?
7. Do you live in Centerville?
8. Are you going to read about Centerville?

CONVERSATIONS

Memorize these conversations. Then go through them with other students.

1 A. Good morning!
   B. Good morning! How are you?
   A. I'm fine, thank you. How are you?
   B. I'm fine, thank you.

2 A. Is that a store?
   B. Yes, it is.
   A. Is that large building a store, too?
   B. No, it isn't. That building is a school.

3   A. Excuse me.
    B. Yes?
    A. What is this?
    B. It's a shirt.
    A. Is that a shirt, too?
    B. No, it isn't. That's a dress.
    A. Oh. Thank you very much.
    B. You're welcome.

GRAMMAR NOTES

1. *THIS* AND *THAT*

This and *that* are pointing words. They are used to point out a person or object. *This* is used when the person or object is near the speaker. *That* is used when the person or object is far from the speaker.

2. SINGULAR AND PLURAL

English has singular and plural forms. *This, that, is* and *a* are usually singular forms. They are used when one person or thing (or one group of persons or things) is spoken about. When two or more things or groups of things are spoken about we use plural forms. You will study some of these plural forms in the next lesson.

3. CONTRACTIONS

Some words or combinations of words are often given contracted pronunciations and spellings. Here are some examples:

LONG FORM	CONTRACTION
I am	I'm
it is	it's
that is	that's
you are	you're
it is not	it isn't

In this book we will often use contractions because these contractions more nearly represent the way the words are spoken in ordinary conversation. In certain formal situations contractions are not used.

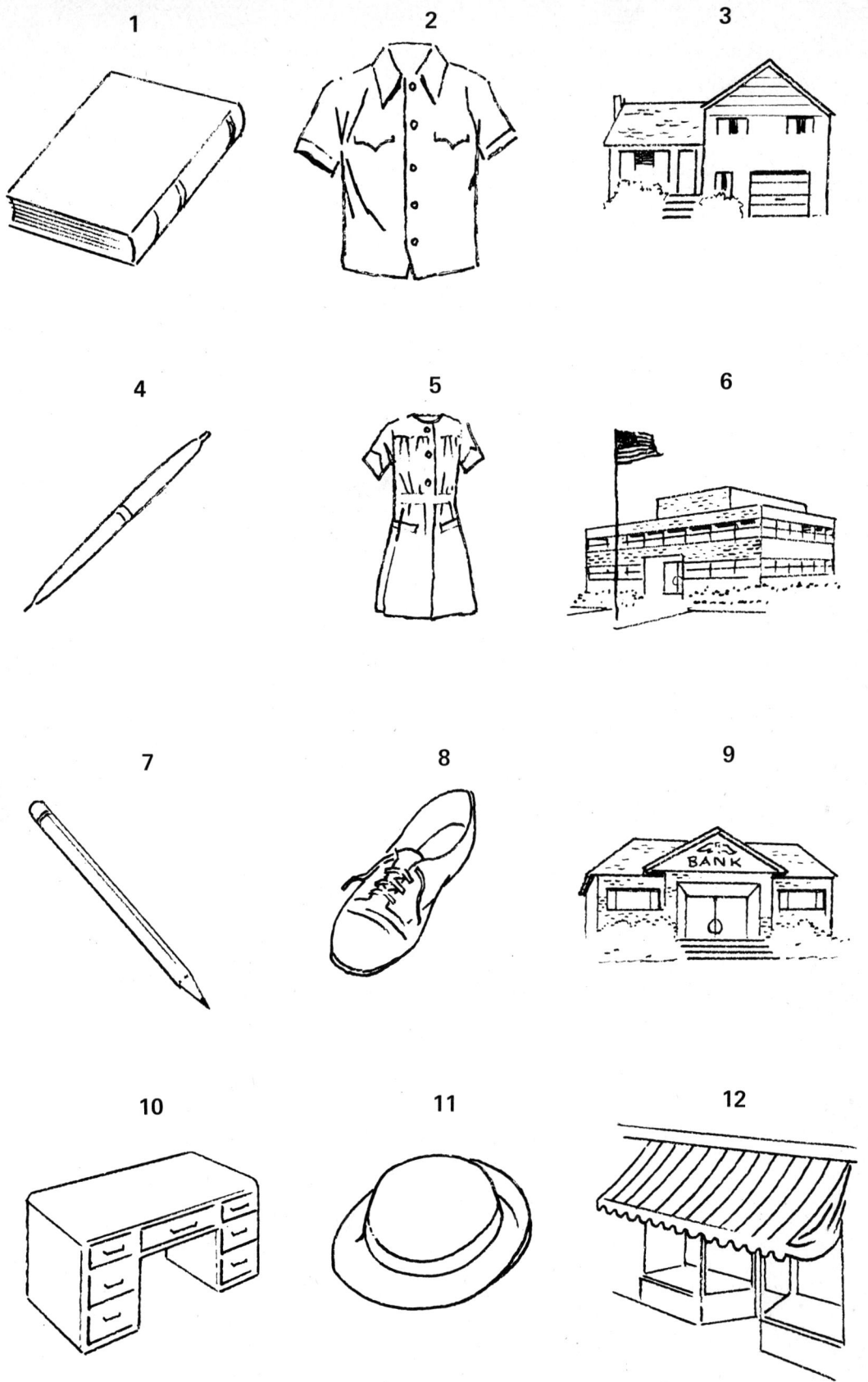

PICTURE DRILLS

(Your teacher will help you practice sentence patterns and pronunciation with these drills.)

1 Practice the numbers from 1 to 12.

1. one	5. five	9. nine
2. two	6. six	10. ten
3. three	7. seven	11. eleven
4. four	8. eight	12. twelve

2 Practice the names of the things in the pictures.

1. book	7. pencil
2. shirt	8. shoe
3. house	9. bank
4. pen	10. desk
5. dress	11. hat
6. school	12. store

3 Practice statements with *this* and the linking verb *is*.

(This is used when things are near the speaker. The pictures should be near the person who is speaking in this drill.)

1. This is a book.	3. This is a house.
2. This is a shirt.	4. This is a pen.
(Continue.)	

4 Practice questions with *this* and *is*.

(The pictures should be near the questioner.)

1. Is this a book?
2. Is this a shirt?
3. Is this a house?
   (Continue.)

5 Practice questions with affirmative answers.

(The questioner should be near the pictures. The one who answers may be near or some distance away.)

1. Is this a book?	Yes, it is.
2. Is this a shirt?	Yes, it is.
3. Is this a house?	Yes, it is.
(Continue.)	

6 Practice questions with negative answers.

(See note for drill 5, above.)

1. Is this a desk?	No, it isn't.
2. Is this a school?	No, it isn't.
3. Is this a shoe?	No, it isn't.
(*Continue.*)	

7 Practice questions with either affirmative or negative answers.

(See note for drill 5, above.)

1. Is this a desk?	No, it isn't.
2. Is this a book?	Yes, it is.
3. Is this a shirt?	Yes, it is.
4. Is this a store?	No, it isn't.
(*Continue.*)	

8 Practice statements with *that*.

(The speaker should be some distance away from the pictures.)

1. That is a book.
2. That is a shirt.
3. That is a house.
   (*Continue.*)

9 Practice questions with *that*.

(The speaker should be some distance away from the pictures.)

1. Is that a book?
2. Is that a shirt?
3. Is that a house?
   (*Continue.*)

10 Practice questions with *that* and affirmative or negative answers.

(The questioner should be some distance away from the pictures. The one who answers may be near or far.)

1. Is that a book?	Yes, it is.
2. Is that a shoe?	No, it isn't.
3. Is that a house?	Yes, it is.
(*Continue.*)	

11 Contrast statements with *this* **and** *that*.

(Place the pictures in various places around the room. Use this *when standing near the pictures and* that *when standing some distance away.)*

1. This is a house.
2. That is a shirt.
3. That is a dress.
4. This is a store.
   (Continue.)

12 Contrast *this* **and** *that* **in questions with short answers.**

(See note for drill 11 above.)

1. Is this a book?	Yes, it is.
2. Is that a book?	No, it isn't.
3. Is that a dress?	Yes, it is.
4. Is this a shirt?	Yes, it is.
(Continue.)	

13 Near or Far?

(The teacher will make statements with this *or* that. *Decide if the thing talked about is near or far.)*

TEACHER	STUDENT
This is a book.	near
This is a house.	near
That is a shirt.	far
This is a pen.	near
(Continue.)	

14 Statement or Question?

(The teacher will say sentences. Decide if the sentence is a statement or a question. Say "statement" if the sentence is a statement. Say "question" if the sentence is a question.)

TEACHER	STUDENT
This is a book.	statement
Is this a book?	question
Is that a pencil?	question
That is a dress.	statement
(Continue.)	

SUBSTITUTION DRILLS

(In these drills, words instead of pictures are used to practice sentence patterns. Your teacher will show you how to practice these drills.)

1 Practice statements with *this* referring to things near the speaker. Follow the examples.

Examples: book   *This is a book.*
            house   *This is a house.*

1. shirt   7. shoe
2. house   8. bank
3. pen   9. school
4. dress   10. house
5. school   11. town
6. pencil   12. family

2 Practice statements with *that* referring to things far from the speaker. Follow the examples.

Examples: school   *That is a school.*
            store   *That is a store.*

1. bank   7. shoe
2. school   8. hat
3. store   9. house
4. bank   10. school
5. family   11. pen
6. town   12. store

3 Practice questions with *this.* Follow the examples.

Examples: book   *Is this a book?*
            pen   *Is this a pen?*

1. desk   7. store
2. hat   8. school
3. store   9. house
4. pencil   10. town
5. shoe   11. family
6. bank   12. house

4 Practice questions with *that.* Follow the examples.

Examples: school   *Is that a school?*
            bank   *Is that a bank?*

1. hat   7. school
2. shoe   8. house
3. dress   9. family
4. shirt   10. town
5. store   11. bank
6. bank   12. school

TRANSFORMATION DRILLS

(In these drills you change sentences from one pattern to another. These drills help you understand the mechanics of English sentence construction.)

1 Change from near to far. Change *this* to *that.*

Example: NEAR   This is a book.
             FAR   *That is a book.*

1. This is a desk.   5. This is a house.
2. This is a shirt.   6. This is a store.
3. This is a family.   7. This is a book.
4. This is a town.   8. This is a drill.

2 Change from statements to questions.

Example: STATEMENT   This is a desk.
             QUESTION   *Is this a desk?*

1. This is a pen.   6. This is a hat.
2. This is a hat.   7. This is a dress.
3. That is a school.   8. That is a town.
4. That is a bank.   9. That is a store.
5. This is a book.   10. This is a drill.

WRITING PRACTICE

Choose one word for each space in the following paragraph. Write the word in the book or on a separate answer sheet according to your teacher's instructions. Be sure to choose just *one* word for each space.

Centerville is a town in the United States. It is a large (1)_____. It has a lot of buildings. One (2)_____ is a bank. Another building (3)_____ a store. Another is a supermarket. Another is a garage. One large (4)_____ is a school. One small building is a house. It is the Bakers' (5)_____. You are going to (6)_____ about the Bakers and about Centerville, too.

SITUATIONAL PRACTICE

(Situational practice gives you a chance to use your English in a meaningful way. It gives you the opportunity to use English for actual communication rather than just in mechanical repetition and drill. Your teacher will help you practice following the suggestions given here.)

1 One student goes to the front of the room, picks up a picture card and asks a question with *this.* Other students answer the questions.

Examples: Student A: "Is this a book?"
              Student B: "Yes, it is."

Student A: "Is this a pen?"
Student C: "No, it isn't."
(*Continue.*)

2 Follow the directions for 1 above but use real objects in the room rather than pictures. If you have mastered the vocabulary for this lesson, your teacher may teach you the names of other things in the room and you can practice with new words.

3 Follow the directions for 1 and 2 above but stand away from the picture or object, point to it with your finger and ask questions with *that*.

Examples: Student A: "Is that a book?"
Student B: "Yes, it is."

Student A: "Is that a shirt?"
Student C: "No, it isn't."
(*Continue.*)

Lesson Two

The Bakers' House

LISTENING DRILL

Step 1. Listen to your teacher pronounce the words below several times.
Step 2. Listen to your teacher say each word and decide if it is number 1, 2, or 3.
Step 3. Answer with the number when the teacher pronounces the words.

1	2	3
eat	it	ate

READING

You remember the Baker family. They live in Centerville. Centerville is a town in the United States. It is a large town. It has a lot of buildings. One of the buildings is the Bakers' house.

The Bakers' house has six rooms. It has a living room, a dining room and a kitchen. It has three bedrooms and one bathroom.

There are six people in the Baker family; Mr. Baker, Mrs. Baker, and their four children.

"YES OR NO" QUESTIONS

Give the correct answer, "Yes, it is", "No, it isn't", "Yes, they do", "No, they don't", etc.

1. Is Centerville in the United States?
2. Is Centerville in England?
3. Is Centerville a small town?
4. Is Centerville a large town?
5. Do the Bakers live in Centerville?
6. Do the Bakers have a house?
7. Does the house have ten rooms?
8. Does the house have six rooms?

CONVERSATIONS

1   A. Good afternoon.
     B. Good afternoon. How are you today?
     A. I'm fine, thank you. How are you?
     B. I'm fine, thank you.
     A. It's a nice day, isn't it?
     B. Yes, it is.

2   A. Are these pencils?
     B. Yes, they are.
     A. Are those pencils too?
     B. No, they aren't. They're pens.
     A. Oh, I understand. Thank you very much.

3   A. Excuse me.
    B. Yes?
    A. What are these?
    B. They're shirts.
    A. Is that a shirt, too?
    B. No, it isn't. It's a dress.
    A. Oh yes, I understand. Thank you.
    B. You're welcome.

GRAMMAR NOTES

1. THESE AND THOSE

These and *those* are pointing words like *this* and *that*. *These* is the plural form of *this*. *Those* is the plural form of *that*. We use *these* and *those* when we are speaking of more than one thing or groups of things. This list will help you remember these pointing words:

Singular near	*this*	Plural near	*these*
Singular far	*that*	Plural far	*those*

2. IS AND ARE

Is is singular. *Are* is usually plural. We use *are* when we are speaking of more than one thing or more than one group of things. Notice these examples:

SINGULAR	PLURAL
This is a book.	These are books.
That is a store.	Those are stores.
Is this a book?	Are these books?
Yes, it is.	Yes, they are.
No, it isn't.	No, they aren't.

3. A

A is a singular word. It is not used when we are speaking about more than one thing. Notice these examples:

SINGULAR	PLURAL
This is a book.	These are books.
That is a desk.	These are desks.

4. CONTRACTIONS WITH ARE

Are is often written in a contracted (shortened) form. The contraction more nearly represents the way the words are generally spoken. Notice these examples:

REGULAR SPELLING		CONTRACTION
They are books.		They're books.
They are shirts.		They're shirts.
Yes, they are.		(no contraction)
No, they are not.		No, they aren't.
	or:	No, they're not.

5. PRONUNCIATION OF PLURAL FORMS

Most plural nouns in English are made by adding *s* to the singular form. (Sometimes a small change in spelling is made when the *s* is added.)

This plural *s* is pronounced in three different ways depending on the sound that comes before it. Here are the three plural *s* sounds with the nouns that you have studied:

1) *s* pronounced /s/

book	books
shirt	shirts
bank	banks
desk	desks
hat	hats

2) *s* pronounced /z/

pen	pens
school	schools
pencil	pencils
shoe	shoes
store	stores

3) *s* pronounced /iz/

house	houses
dress	dresses
class	classes

Listen to the teacher pronounce these plural forms several times. Then practice deciding which of the three forms you hear. When the teacher says the word the students respond with the number, 1, 2, or 3. Then repeat the words after the teacher. Be careful to use the correct pronunciation of the plural forms when you are doing the drills and conversations.

The rules which explain the pronunciation of the plural *s* are:

1. If the sound before the plural *s* is a sibilant (*dress, cheese, wash, watch, wedge*), the plural *s* is pronounced /iz/ (*dresses, cheeses, washes, watches, wedges*).

2. If the sound before the *s* is not a sibilant, the plural *s* is pronounced /s/ after an unvoiced sound and /z/ after a voiced sound. See lists 1 and 2, above, for some examples.

Although these rules may seem a little complicated, you will find that you can easily give the correct pronunciation of the plural *s* after you become familiar with the language.

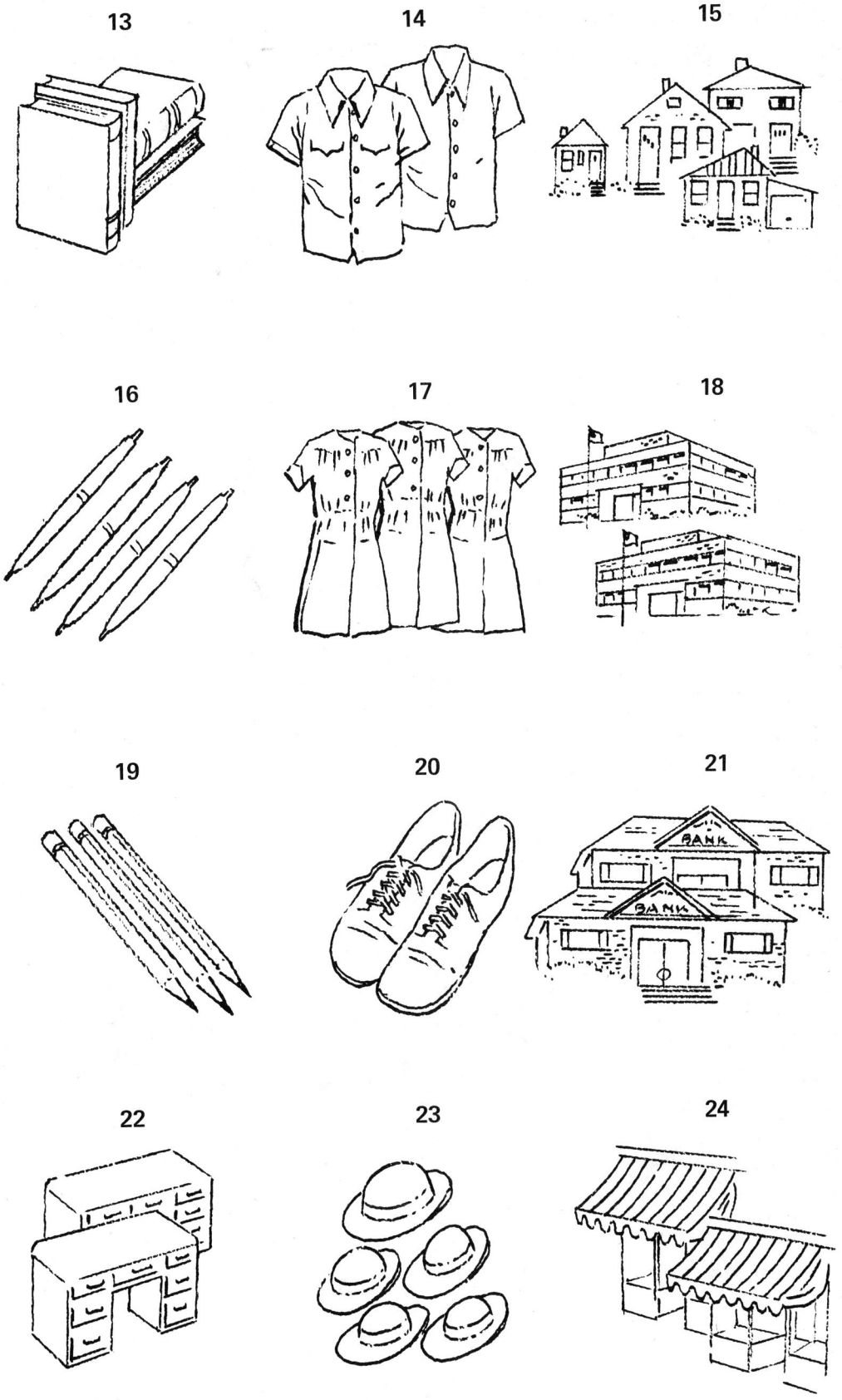

13

14

15

16

17

18

19

20

21

22

23

24

PICTURE DRILLS

1 Review the numbers 1 to 12.

2 Practice the numbers 13 to 24.

13. thirteen	17. seventeen	21. twenty-one
14. fourteen	18. eighteen	22. twenty-two
15. fifteen	19. nineteen	23. twenty-three
16. sixteen	20. twenty	24. twenty-four

3 Practice the plural forms of nouns.

books /s/	shirts /s/	houses /iz/
pens /z/	dresses /iz/	schools /z/
pencils /z/	shoes /z/	banks /s/
desks /s/	hats /s/	stores /z/

4 Practice the plural forms in statements with *these*.

(The pictures should be near the speaker.)

1. These are books.
2. These are shirts.
3. These are houses.
4. These are pens.
    (*Continue.*)

5 Practice questions with *these* and affirmative answers.

(The pictures should be near the questioner.)

1. Are these books?	Yes, they are.
2. Are these shirts?	Yes, they are.
3. Are these houses?	Yes, they are.
4. Are these pens?	Yes, they are.
(*Continue.*)	

6 Practice questions with *these* and negative answers.

(The pictures should be near the questioner.)

1. Are these stores?	No, they aren't.
2. Are these hats?	No, they aren't.
3. Are these desks?	No, they aren't.
(*Continue.*)	

7 Ask questions with *these* **and force a choice between affirmative and negative answers.**

(The pictures should be near the questioner.)

1. Are these books?	Yes, they are.
2. Are these shoes?	No, they aren't.
3. Are these pencils?	No, they aren't.
4. Are these pens?	Yes, they are.
(Continue.)	

8 Practice statements with *those.*

(The pictures should be far from the speaker.)

1. Those are books.
2. Those are shirts.
3. Those are houses.
4. Those are pens.
   (Continue.)

9 Practice questions with *those.*

(The pictures should be far from the questioner.)

1. Are those books?
2. Are those shirts?
3. Are those houses?
4. Are those pens?
   (Continue.)

10 Practice questions with *those* **and force a choice between affirmative and negative answers.**

(The pictures should be far from the questioner. They may be near to or far from the person who answers.)

1. Are those books?	Yes, they are.
2. Are those hats?	No, they aren't.
3. Are those houses?	Yes, they are.
(Continue.)	

11 Review *this* **with singular forms.**

(Use the picture cards for Lesson One. Have the pictures near the speaker.)

1. This is a book.
2. This is a shirt.
3. This is a house.
   (Continue.)

12 Review *that* with singular forms.

(Place the picture cards for Lesson One far from the speaker.)

1. That is a book.
2. That is a shirt.
3. That is a house.
   (Continue.)

13 Contrast the use of *this* and *these*.

(Use picture cards from both Lesson One and Lesson Two near the speaker.)

1. This is a book.
2. These are books.
3. This is a shirt.
4. These are shirts.
   (Continue.)

14 Contrast *this* with *these* in questions and *it* with *they* in answers.

(The picture cards from Lessons One and Two should be near the questioner. They may be near or far from the person who answers.)

1. Is this a book?	Yes, it is.
2. Is this a desk?	No, it isn't.
3. Are these houses?	Yes, they are.
4. Are these shoes?	No, they aren't.
5. Is this a hat?	Yes, it is.
(Continue.)	

15 Singular or Plural?

Decide if the nouns (and other related words) are singular or plural.

TEACHER	STUDENTS
This is a book.	singular
These are books.	plural
Those are shirts.	plural
This is a house.	singular
That is a desk.	singular

16 Statement or Question?

Decide if the sentences that the teacher says are statements or questions.

TEACHER	STUDENTS
This is a house.	statement
These are shirts.	statement

Are these houses?   question
Is this a desk?   question
That is a shoe.   statement
(*Continue.*)

17 *Near* or *Far*?

Decide if the teacher is talking about things that are near or things that are far.

TEACHER	STUDENTS
This is a book.	near
That is a shirt.	far
Those are houses.	far
These are pens.	near
This is a dress.	near
(*Continue.*)	

SUBSTITUTION DRILLS

1 Practice statements with *these* referring to things near the speaker. Follow the example.

Example: desks   *These are desks.*

1. books	7. shirts
2. shirts	8. shoes
3. houses	9. dresses
4. rooms	10. hats
5. bedrooms	11. houses
6. beds	12. bathrooms

2 Review statements with *this* referring to something near the speaker. Follow the example.

Example: desk   *This is a desk.*

1. book	7. room
2. pen	8. living room
3. pencil	9. dining room
4. desk	10. kitchen
5. shirt	11. bedroom
6. dress	12. bathroom

3 Contrast *this* and *these* using singular and plural forms. Follow the examples.

Examples: pen   *This is a pen.*
                    pens *These are pens.*

1. house	4. schools
2. houses	5. bank
3. school	6. banks

7. room   10. bedrooms
8. rooms   11. beds
9. bedroom   12. bed

4 Practice statements with *those* referring to things far from the speaker. Follow the example.

Example: banks   *Those are banks.*

1. rooms	7. stores
2. bedrooms	8. sentences
3. bathrooms	9. statements
4. beds	10. questions
5. shoes	11. answers
6. schools	12. towns

5 Review statements with *that* referring to something far from the speaker. Follow the example.

Example: bank   *That is a bank.*

1. house	7. bank
2. room	8. answer
3. store	9. living room
4. town	10. dining room
5. sentence	11. kitchen
6. statement	12. bathroom

6 Contrast *that* and *those* using singular and plural forms. Follow the examples.

Examples: pen   *That is a pen.*
                pens   *Those are pens.*

1. room	7. bank
2. rooms	8. schools
3. house	9. town
4. houses	10. towns
5. sentences	11. answers
6. sentence	12. answer

TRANSFORMATION DRILLS

1 Change from singular to plural. Change *this* to *these*. Change *that* to *those*. Follow the examples.

Examples: Singular   This is a book.
                 Plural   *These are books.*

                       Singular   That is a pen.
                       Plural   *Those are pens.*

1. This is a room.	3. This is a pen.
2. That is a bedroom.	4. This is a shoe.

5. This is a house.
6. That is a store.
7. That is a school.

8. That is a desk.
9. This is a store.
10. This is a drill.

2 Change from near to far. Change *this* **or** *these* **(near) to** *that* **or** *those* **(far). Follow the examples.**

Examples:	Near	This is a bank.
	Far	*That is a bank.*
	Near	These are stores.
	Far	*Those are stores.*

1. This is a room.
2. These are rooms.
3. This is a living room.
4. These are living rooms.
5. This is a town.

6. These are towns.
7. This is a house.
8. These are houses.
9. This is a drill.
10. These are drills.

3 Change from statements to questions. Follow the example.

Example:	Statement	This is a pencil.
	Question	*Is this a pencil?*

1. This is a shirt.
2. That is a house.
3. These are shirts.
4. Those are houses.
5. This is a dress.

6. This is a store.
7. That is a shoe.
8. Those are shoes.
9. Those are drills.
10. This is a sentence.

WRITING PRACTICE

Choose one word for each space in this paragraph. Write the word in the book or on a separate answer sheet according to your teacher's instructions. Choose just *one* word for each space.

You remember the Baker family. They live in (1)_____. Centerville (2)_____ a town in the United States. It is a large (3)_____ . It has a lot of buildings. One of the buildings is the Bakers' (4)_____ . The Bakers' house has six rooms. It has a living (5)_____ , a dining room and a kitchen. It has three (6)_____ and one bathroom.

SITUATIONAL PRACTICE

1 Use the picture cards from Lesson Two. Go to the front of the room, pick up a picture card and ask a question with *these*. **Ask another student to answer.**

Example:	Student A:	(Goes to front of room and picks up picture of books.)
		"Are these books?"
	Student B:	"Yes, they are."

> Student A: (Picks up picture of shoes.)
>   "Are these hats?"
> Student C: "No, they aren't."
> (*Continue.*)

2 Put some of the picture cards where everybody can see them. Stand away from the pictures and ask questions with *those.* Let other students answer. Continue as in 1.

3 Use picture cards from both Lesson One and Lesson Two. First stand near the cards and ask questions with *this* and *these.* Then stand away from the cards and ask questions with *that* and *those.* Let other students answer. Continue as in 1 and 2.

4 Use real things in your classroom. Walk around the room and make statements such as: "This is a desk.", "This is a door.", "This is a window." Then stand away from the things, point to them and make statements with *that* or *those:* "That is a table.", "Those are chairs." Your teacher may tell you the English names of more of the things in your classroom.

5 Proceed as in 4 but ask questions instead of making statements. Ask other students to answer your questions.

Lesson Three

Things in the House

LISTENING DRILL

Step 1. Listen to your teacher pronounce the words below several times.

Step 2. Listen to your teacher say each word and decide if it is number 1, 2, 3, or 4.

Step 3. Answer with the number when the teacher pronounces the words.

1	2	3	4
beat	bit	bait	bet

READING

The Bakers live in Centerville. They live in a house. The house has six rooms. It has a living room, a dining room, a kitchen, three bedrooms, and a bathroom.

The Bakers have a lot of things in their house. They have chairs, tables, beds, a sofa, a TV set, and many other things. In the kitchen they have a stove, a refrigerator, a sink, and some cabinets. In the bathroom there is a toilet, a sink, and a bathtub.

Mrs. Baker has a lot of dishes. She has plates, cups, glasses, knives, forks, spoons, pots, pans, and many other things.

In this lesson you are going to practice with the names of things in the house.

"YES OR NO" QUESTIONS

Give the correct answer, "Yes, it is", "No, it isn't", "Yes, they do", "No, they don't", etc.

1. Do the Bakers live in a house in Centerville?
2. Does the house have six rooms?
3. Does the house have three bathrooms?
4. Do the Bakers have a TV set?
5. Does Mrs. Baker have a lot of dishes?
6. Is Centerville a small town?
7. Is Centerville a large town?
8. Is Centerville in the United States?

CONVERSATIONS

1   A. Hi, how are you today?
    B. I'm fine, thanks. How are you?
    A. I'm fine, thanks.
    B. Today is Wednesday, isn't it?
    A. Yes, it is. Tomorrow is Thursday.

2   A. What is this?
    B. It's a chair.
    A. Is that a chair, too?

B. No, it isn't. That's a sofa.
A. What are these?
B. They're tables.

3 A. Is this a knife?
   B. No, it isn't a knife. It's a fork.
   A. Oh . . . what is this?
   B. It's a spoon.
   A. What are these things?
   B. They're plates, cups, and glasses.
   A. I see. Thank you very much.
   B. You're welcome.

GRAMMAR NOTES

1. WHAT

What is a question word. It is often used to ask questions about things. There are several other question words in English. You will study these later. Question words do not change form in English. There is no change for singular and plural. Notice these examples:

What is this?	What are these?
What is that?	What are those?
What day is today?	What day is tomorrow?

2. NEGATIVE STATEMENTS

Statements can be affirmative or negative. We usually make a negative statement by putting *not* after the verb. We often use the contraction of *not* which is *n't*. Notice these examples:

Affirmative	This is a spoon.	These are spoons.
Negative	This is not a spoon.	These are not spoons.
Contraction	This isn't a spoon.	These aren't spoons.

Affirmative	Centerville is a town.
Negative	Centerville is not a city.
Contraction	Centerville isn't a city.

3. DAYS OF THE WEEK

There are seven days in a week. The English names of the days are:

Sunday
Monday
Tuesday
Wednesday
Thursday
Friday
Saturday

Most people in the United States work or go to school five days a week: Monday, Tuesday, Wednesday, Thursday, and Friday. These days are called *weekdays.* Saturday and Sunday are called the *weekend.*

4. THE ALPHABET

There are 26 letters in the English alphabet. Each letter has a name. The name of the letter is not exactly the same as the sound of the letter when it is used in a word. You need to learn the names of the letters so that you can spell your name and other words out loud.

Here are the first eight letters of the alphabet. Practice pronouncing the names of these letters by repeating them after your teacher:

A   B   C   D   E   F   G   H

5. *KNIFE—KNIVES*

The plural of *knife* is *knives*. The "f" changes to a "v". This change happens with several words in English. Another example is *wife—wives*. You will learn other words that change in this way later.

6. PLURALS (REVIEW)

Most plural nouns are formed by adding *s* to the singular form. This *s* may be pronounced in three different ways: /s/, /z/ or /iz/.

A few nouns have irregular plural forms. In this lesson, for example, we have the word *knife* whose plural form is *knives*. You will learn these irregular plural forms as you become more familiar with the language.

Other words in a sentence change form according to whether the subject noun is singular or plural. In these first two lessons you have practiced with these changes:

USED WITH SINGULAR SUBJECT	*USED WITH PLURAL SUBJECT*
it	they
is	are
this	these
that	those

25

26

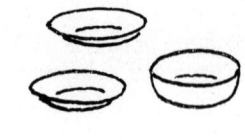

27

28

29

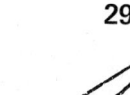
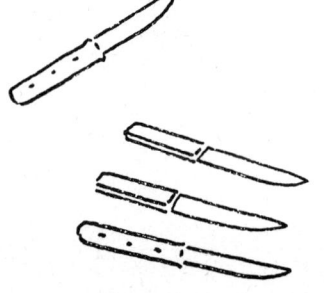

30

31

32

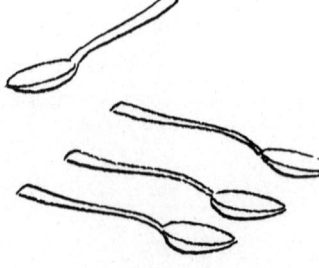

PICTURE DRILLS

1 Review the numbers from 1 to 24 using the pictures from Lessons One and Two.

2 Practice the numbers from 25 to 32.

25	twenty-five	29	twenty-nine
26	twenty-six	30	thirty
27	twenty-seven	31	thirty-one
28	twenty-eight	32	thirty-two

3 Practice the singular form of the things in the pictures.

cup	bowl
fork	glass
knife	pan
plate	spoon

4 Practice the plural forms of the things in the pictures.

cups	/s/	bowls	/z/
forks	/s/	glasses	/iz/
knives	/z/	pans	/z/
plates	/s/	spoons	/z/

5 Practice statements with *it* and singular forms.

1. It is a cup.
2. It is a bowl.
3. It is a fork.
   (*Continue.*)

6 Practice questions with *what* and answers with *it* and singular forms.

(*The person who asks the questions should be near the items or picture cards.*)

1. What is this?	It is a cup.
2. What is this?	It is a bowl.
3. What is this?	It is a fork.
(*Continue.*)	

7 Practice statements with *they* using plural forms.

1. They are cups.
2. They are bowls.
3. They are forks.
   (*Continue.*)

8 Practice questions with *what* and answers with *they* and other plural forms.

(The person who asks the questions should be near the items or picture cards.)

1. What are these?	They are cups.
2. What are these?	They are bowls.
3. What are these?	They are forks.
(Continue.)	

9 Contrast the singular and plural forms.

1. What is this?	It is a cup.
2. What are these?	They are cups.
3. What is this?	It is a bowl.
4. What are these?	They are bowls.
5. What are these?	They are forks.
(Continue.)	

10 Practice questions and answers using *that* and *those*.

(The person who asks the questions should move away from the items or picture cards and point toward them for this drill.)

1. What is that?	It is a cup.
2. What are those?	They are cups.
3. What are those?	They are bowls.
4. What is that?	It is a fork.
(Continue.)	

11 Review "Yes or No" questions and short answers.

(The person who asks the questions should be near the pictures.)

1. Is this a cup?	Yes, it is.
2. Are these cups?	Yes, they are.
3. Is this a house?	No, it isn't.
4. Are these houses?	No, they aren't.
(Continue.)	

12 Contrast "Yes or No" questions with question-word questions.

1. What is this?	It is a cup.
2. What are these?	They are cups.
3. Are these bowls?	Yes, they are.
4. Are these pans?	No, they aren't.
5. Is this a bank?	No, it isn't.
6. What is this?	It's a fork.
(Continue.)	

13 Contrast singular and plural.

TEACHER	STUDENTS
What is this?	singular
What are these?	plural
It is a cup.	singular
They are cups.	plural
These are bowls.	plural
That is a knife.	singular
That is a spoon.	singular
(*Continue.*)	

14 Contrast "near" and "far".

TEACHER	STUDENTS
This is a cup.	near
That is a bowl.	far
What is that?	far
What is this?	near
What is that?	far
Is this a knife?	near
Are these knives?	near
(*Continue.*)	

15 Contrast affirmative and negative.

TEACHER	STUDENTS
This is a cup.	affirmative
This isn't a bowl.	negative
These are bowls.	affirmative
These aren't hats.	negative
This isn't a dress.	negative
Those are houses.	affirmative
That is a bank.	affirmative
(*Continue.*)	

SUBSTITUTION DRILLS

1 Practice questions with *what* and singular and plural pointing words (*this*, *that*, *these*, and *those*). Follow the examples.

Examples:	this	*What is this?*
	these	*What are these?*

1. this	5. that
2. that	6. those
3. these	7. this
4. those	8. these

2 Practice affirmative statements with *it* and singular forms. Follow the example.

Example: book   *It is a book.*

1. spoon	8. sofa
2. knife	9. chair
3. glass	10. TV set
4. fork	11. table
5. cup	12. sink
6. bathtub	13. house
7. kitchen	14. room

3 Practice affirmative statements with *they* and plural forms. Follow the example.

Example: books   *They are books.*

1. forks	8. tables
2. spoons	9. stoves
3. knives	10. bathtubs
4. glasses	11. rooms
5. pans	12. kitchens
6. plates	13. towns
7. chairs	14. sofas

4 Practice negative statements with *it* and singular forms. Follow the example.

Example: bank   *It isn't a bank.*

1. pen	8. hat
2. house	9. shoe
3. store	10. fork
4. school	11. spoon
5. shirt	12. house
6. dress	13. small house
7. desk	14. small town

5 Practice negative statements with *they* and plural forms. Follow the example.

Example: chairs   *They aren't chairs.*

1. tables	8. pencils
2. desks	9. pens
3. sinks	10. stores
4. stoves	11. houses
5. bathtubs	12. banks
6. questions	13. sofas
7. books	14. affirmative statements

6 Contrast singular and plural forms in negative statements. Follow the examples.

Examples: chair   *It isn't a chair.*
            chairs *They aren't chairs.*

1. pen
2. pens
3. desk
4. fork
5. spoon
6. glass
7. forks
8. spoons
9. glasses
10. cup
11. question
12. questions

7 Practice the pattern of related statements with singular forms. Make the first statement negative and the second statement affirmative. Follow the example.

Example: cup/bowl *It isn't a cup. It is a bowl.*

1. pen/pencil
2. knife/fork
3. cup/bowl
4. bowl/pan
5. fork/spoon
6. shirt/dress
7. school/bank
8. table/desk
9. question/statement
10. small town/large town

8 Practice the pattern of related statements with plural forms. Make the first statement negative and the second affirmative. Follow the example.

Example: cups/bowls *They aren't cups.*
                          They are bowls.

1. pens/pencils
2. knives/forks
3. cups/bowls
4. bowls/pans
5. forks/spoons
6. shirts/dresses
7. schools/banks
8. tables/desks
9. questions/statements
10. small towns/large towns

TRANSFORMATION DRILLS

1 Change from singular to plural. Follow the example.

Example: Singular It is a cup.
            Plural   *They are cups.*

1. It is a chair.
2. It is a stove.
3. It is a sofa.
4. It is a TV set.
5. It is a table.
6. It is a chair.
7. This is a chair.
8. This is a bathtub.
9. That is a house.
10. That is a bank.
11. What is this?
12. What is that?

2 Change from affirmative to negative. Follow the examples.

> Examples: Affirmative   It is a chair.
> Negative   *It isn't a chair.*
>
> Affirmative   They are desks.
> Negative   *They aren't desks.*

1. It is a book.
2. They are pens.
3. They are cups.
4. It is a table.
5. This is a house.
6. That is a bank.
7. These are books.
8. Those are desks.
9. It is a town.
10. It is a small town
11. They are questions.
12. These are plural statements.

3 Change from statements to questions. Follow the example.

> Example: Statement   This is a cup.
> Question   *Is this a cup?*

1. This is a chair.
2. That is a bed.
3. These are spoons.
4. Those are knives.
5. It is a bank.
6. They are banks.
7. Centerville is a town.
8. Centerville is a large town.
9. It is in the United States.
10. These are English sentences.

WRITING PRACTICE

8 Choose one word for each space in the paragraphs.

The Bakers live (1)_____Centerville. They live in a house. The (2)_____ has six rooms. It has a living room, a dining (3)_____, a kitchen, three bedrooms, and a bathroom. The Bakers have a lot of things in their (4)_____ . They have chairs, tables, beds, a sofa, a TV set, and many other things. In the kitchen, they have a (5)_____ , a refrigerator, a sink, and some cabinets. In the bathroom there is a toilet, a sink, and a (6)_____ .

SITUATIONAL PRACTICE

1 Use the charts or picture cards for Lessons One, Two, and Three. Go to the front of the room, pick up a card and ask another student a question. Use the question-word *what.* Have the student answer using *it* or *they.*

> Examples: "What is this?"   "It is a cup."
> "What are these?"   "They are books."

2 Go to the front of the room and pick up a picture card but don't let the other students see it. Ask, "What is this?" (or "What are these?"). Let other students guess by asking, "Is it a cup?", "Is it a pen?" etc. The student who guesses the right answer then goes to the front of the room and the game begins again.

Example: Student A: (Goes to front of room, picks up a card, looks at
                                the picture but doesn't let the class see it.)
                                "What is this?"
                Student B: "Is it a book?"
                Student A: "No, it isn't."
                Student C: "Is it a pen?"
                Student A: "No, it isn't."
                Student D: "Is it a bowl?"
                Student A: "Yes, it is."
                Student D: (Goes to front of room, picks up a card and the
                                game continues)

Practice using both singular and plural forms.

3 Walk around the room asking questions with *what:* "What is this?", "What are these?" Let the
other students answer your questions. If you have learned the words in the first three lessons
fairly well, your teacher may teach you the names of more things in the room.

Lesson Four

The Baker Family

LISTENING DRILL

Step 1. Listen to your teacher pronounce the words below several times.

Step 2. Listen to your teacher say each word and decide if it is number 1, 2, 3, or 4.

Step 3. Answer with the number when the teacher pronounces the words.

1	2	3	4
bit	bait	bet	bat

READING

You remember the Baker family. They have a fairly large house in Centerville. The house has six rooms. It has a living room, a dining room, a kitchen, three bedrooms, and a bathroom. The Bakers have a lot of things in their house. They have a TV set, a sofa, chairs, tables, a stove, a refrigerator, and many other things. Mrs. Baker has a lot of dishes. She has plates, cups, glasses, knives, forks, spoons, pots, pans, and other things.

There are six people in the Baker family: Mr. Baker, Mrs. Baker, and four children. The children's names are Joan, Peter, Tom, and Carol. There are two boys and two girls. Peter and Tom are boys. Joan and Carol are girls.

You are going to practice with the names of the people in the Baker family in this lesson.

"YES OR NO" QUESTIONS

Give the correct answer, "Yes, they do", "No, they don't", "Yes, he is", or "No, he isn't", etc.

1. Do the Bakers have a small house?
2. Do they have a fairly large house?
3. Are there six people in the Baker family?
4. Is Tom a boy?
5. Is Peter a boy?
6. Are Peter and Tom boys?
7. Are Joan and Carol girls?
8. Does Mrs. Baker have a lot of dishes?

CONVERSATIONS

1   A. Who is that?
    B. He is Mr. Baker.
    A. Is he a man?
    B. Yes, he is.
    A. Who is that?
    B. That is Tom Baker.
    A. Is he a man, too?
    B. No, he isn't. He is a boy.

2 A. Who are those boys?
   B. They're Peter and Tom.
   A. Who are those girls?
   B. They're Joan and Carol.
   A. Are they Mr. and Mrs. Baker's children?
   B. Yes, they are.

3 A. Excuse me.
   B. Yes?
   A. Are you Peter Baker?
   B. No, I'm not. I'm _____ .*
   A. Oh, I'm sorry.
   B. That's all right.

GRAMMAR NOTES

1. THE ALPHABET

In Lesson Three you learned the names of these eight letters:

A B C D E F G H

Here are eight more letters:

I J K L M N O P

Practice repeating the names of these letters after your teacher. Remember that the name of the letter is not always the same as its sound in a word. Some letters have different sounds in different words. We use the names of the letters to spell words aloud.

2. SUBJECT PRONOUNS

I, you, he, she, it, we, and *they* are pronouns. In this book we will call them subject pronouns. You have already studied *it* and *they* in Lessons One, Two, and Three. In this lesson you will practice using pronouns that refer to people. Some of these pronouns are singular. Others are plural:

	SINGULAR	*PLURAL*
First Person	I	we
Second Person	you	you
Third Person	he, she, it	they

3. *I AM, YOU ARE, HE IS, SHE IS*

The subject pronouns are followed by certain forms of the linking verb *be* (*am, is, are*). Notice these examples:

SINGULAR	*PLURAL*
I am	we are
you are	you are
he is	they are
she is	
it is	

Notice that *are* which is usually a plural form is always used with *you*, both in the singular and the plural reference.

*Students may use their own names when practicing this conversation individually.

4. CONTRACTIONS WITH SUBJECT PRONOUNS

Contractions are often used with subject pronouns. The affirmative contractions are:

LONG FORM	CONTRACTION
I am	I'm
You are	You're
He is	He's
She is	She's
It is	It's
We are	We're
They are	They're

The contractions of *is* ('s) are easily confused with other forms in English such as the possessive, the plural, and the third person singular of the simple verb form. For this reason we do not use these contractions in this text except in the conversations. However, when you speak you should generally pronounce these forms as if the contraction were given. These "contracted" pronunciations are commonly used in ordinary conversation.

5. NEGATIVE CONTRACTIONS

In this text we will use these negative contractions with subject pronouns:

LONG FORM	CONTRACTION
I am not.	I'm not.*
You are not.	You aren't.
He is not.	He isn't.
She is not.	She isn't.
It is not.	It isn't.
We are not.	We aren't.
They are not.	They aren't.

There are other forms of negative contractions which you will learn later.

6. *WHO?*

In Lesson Three you learned the question-word *what*. *Who* is another question word. *What* generally refers to things. *Who* generally refers to people. Notice these examples:

Who is he?	He is Mr. Baker.
Who is she?	She is Miss Smith.
Who are they?	They are Peter and Joan.

7. *MAN—MEN, WOMAN—WOMEN*

Most plural nouns are made by adding "s" to the singular form, but a few nouns are irregular. *Man* and *woman* form their plurals in an irregular way. The plural of *man* is *men*. The plural of *woman* is *women*.

These spellings do not show the pronunciation of these plural forms clearly. Practice repeating these singular and plural forms after your teacher.

SINGULAR	PLURAL
man	men
woman	women

*There is no contraction of *not* with *am*. Do not use *amn't*. There is no such form in English.

33

Mr. Baker

34

Mrs. Baker

1765053

35

Joan

36

Peter

37

Tom

38

Carol

PICTURE DRILLS

1 Review the numbers 1 to 32 using the illustrations or picture cards from Lessons One, Two, and Three.

2 Practice the numbers from 33 to 38.

33. thirty-three	36. thirty-six
34. thirty-four	37. thirty-seven
35. thirty-five	38. thirty-eight

3 Practice the names in the pictures.

(Remember, the numbers do not refer to the picture numbers.)

1. Mr. Baker	4. Peter
2. Mrs. Baker	5. Tom
3. Joan	6. Carol

4 Practice the names in statements.

1. Mr. Baker is a man.	4. Peter is a boy.
2. Mrs. Baker is a woman.	5. Tom is a boy.
3. Joan is a girl.	6. Carol is a girl.

5 Practice the statements with subject pronouns substituted for the names.

1. He is a man.	4. He is a boy.
2. She is a woman.	5. He is a boy.
3. She is a girl.	6. She is a girl.

6 Practice questions with the names.

1. Is Mr. Baker a man?	4. Is Peter a boy?
2. Is Mrs. Baker a woman?	5. Is Tom a boy?
3. Is Joan a girl?	6. Is Carol a girl?

7 Practice questions with the names and short answers with subject pronouns.

1. Is Mr. Baker a man?	Yes, he is.
2. Is Mrs. Baker a woman?	Yes, she is.
3. Is Joan a girl?	Yes, she is.
4. Is Peter a man?	No, he isn't.
5. Is Peter a boy?	Yes, he is.
6. Is Tom a boy?	Yes, he is.
7. Are Peter and Tom boys?	Yes, they are.
8. Are Joan and Carol girls?	Yes, they are.
9. Are Peter and Tom men?	No, they aren't.
(Continue.)	

8 Practice questions with *who*.

1. Who is he?   3. Who is he?
2. Who is she?   4. Who are they?
(*Continue.*)

9 Practice questions with *who* and short answers.

1. Who is he?   He is Mr. Baker.
2. Who is she?   She is Mrs. Baker.
3. Who is she?   She is Joan.
4. Who are they?   They are Peter and Tom.
(*Continue.*)

10 True or False? The teacher will point to a picture and make a statement. Decide if the statement is true or false.

TEACHER	STUDENTS
Mr. Baker is a man.	true
Mrs. Baker is a woman.	true
Peter is a man.	false
Joan is a girl.	true
Tom is a man.	
Peter and Tom are boys.	
Peter and Tom are men.	
Carol is a woman.	
Carol is a girl.	
(*Continue.*)	

SUBSTITUTION DRILLS

1 Practice statements with names. Follow the example.

Example: Tom/boy   *Tom is a boy.*

1. Mr. Baker/man
2. Mrs. Baker/woman
3. Joan/girl
4. Peter/boy
5. Tom/boy
6. Carol/girl
7. Joan and Carol/girls
8. Peter and Tom/boys
9. Peter/boy
10. Mr. Baker and Mr. Hill/men

2 Practice statements with subject pronouns. Follow the example.

Example: he/man   *He is a man.*

1. he/man
2. he/boy
3. she/girl
4. she/woman
5. they/boys
6. they/girls
7. they/men
8. they/women
9. he/boy
10. I/_____
11. you/ _____
12. we/students

3 Practice questions with names. Follow the example.

> Example: Mr. Baker/man *Is Mr. Baker a man?*

1. Mrs. Baker/woman	6. Peter and Tom/boys
2. Joan/girl	7. Joan and Carol/girls
3. Peter/boy	8. Mrs. Baker/woman
4. Tom/boy	9. Peter/boy
5. Mr. Baker/man	10. Peter and Tom/boys

4 Practice questions with subject pronouns. Follow the example.

> Example: he/man *Is he a man?*

1. he/boy	7. she/girl
2. you/boy	8. they/girls
3. I/man	9. he/man
4. she/woman	10. you/men
5. they/men	11. she/woman
6. they/boys	12. they/women

5 Practice negative statements with names. Follow the example.

> Example: Mr. Baker/boy *Mr. Baker isn't a boy.*

1. Mrs. Baker/girl	6. Peter and Tom/men
2. Joan/boy	7. Joan and Carol/women
3. Joan/woman	8. Mr. Baker/boy
4. Peter/man	9. Tom/girl
5. Tom/man	10. Peter and Tom/girls

6 Practice negative statements with subject pronouns. Follow the example.

> Example: he/man *He isn't a man.*

1. she/woman	7. she/girl
2. you/boy	8. they/women
3. he/boy	9. he/girl
4. they/boys	10. she/boy
5. they/girls	11. I/_____
6. he/man	12. you/_____

7 Practice patterns of related statements. Make the first statement negative and the second affirmative. Use the name in the first statement and the subject pronoun in the second. Follow the example.

> Example: Mr. Baker/boy/man *Mr. Baker isn't a boy. He is a man.*

1. Mrs. Baker/girl/woman	3. Joan and Carol/women/girls
2. Joan/boy/girl	4. You/?/?

5. Tom/man/boy
6. Peter/man/boy
7. Peter and Tom/men/boys

8. I/_____/_____/
9. We/teachers/students
10. You/student/teacher

8 Practice questions with *who.* Follow the example.

Example: he *Who is he?*

1. he
2. she
3. you
4. they
5. I

6. you
7. they
8. I
9. we
10. she

TRANSFORMATION DRILLS

1 Change the names to subject pronouns in these statements. Follow the example.

Example: Name Mr. Baker is a man.
Pronoun *He is a man.*

1. Mrs. Baker is a woman.
2. Tom is a boy.
3. Carol is a girl.
4. Peter and Tom are boys.

5. Joan and Carol are girls.
6. Mr. Baker is a man.
7. Mr. Baker and Mr. Hill are men.
8. Mrs. Baker and Mrs. Hill are women.

2 Change the names to subject pronouns in these questions. Follow the example.

Example: Name Is Mrs. Baker a woman?
Pronoun *Is she a woman?*

1. Is Mr. Baker a man?
2. Is Tom a boy?
3. Are Peter and Tom boys?
4. Is Carol a girl?
5. Is Joan a girl?

6. Are Carol and Joan girls?
7. Is Peter a boy?
8. Is Mr. Hill a man?
9. Are Mr. Hill and Mr. Baker men?
10. Are Mrs. Hill and Mrs. Baker women?

3 Change the names to subject pronouns in these negative statements. Follow the example.

Example: Name Tom isn't a boy.
Pronoun *He isn't a boy.*

1. Mrs. Baker isn't a girl.
2. Tom isn't a man.
3. Peter isn't a man.
4. Peter and Tom aren't men.
5. Joan isn't a boy.

6. Carol isn't a boy.
7. Joan and Carol aren't boys.
8. Peter and Tom aren't girls.
9. Mr. Hill and Mr. Baker aren't women.
10. Mrs. Hill and Mrs. Baker aren't men.

4 Change these statements to questions. Follow the example.

Example: Statement   He is a boy.
            Question   *Is he a boy?*

1. She is a girl.
2. They are girls.
3. You are a man.
4. We are men.
5. This is a book.
6. These are pencils.
7. That is a cup.
8. Those are cups.

9. It is a school.
10. They are banks.
11. Mrs. Baker is a woman.
12. Centerville is a town.
13. Centerville is a large town.
14. This is an English book.
15. Those are small shoes.
16. This is a large class.

5 Change these statements from affirmative to negative. Follow the example.

Example: Affirmative   He is a boy.
            Negative   *He isn't a boy.*

1. She is a girl.
2. They are girls.
3. I am a man.
4. You are a boy.
5. This is a knife.
6. These are knives.
7. These are bowls.
8. Those are glasses.
9. That is a shirt.
10. Those are shoes.

11. It is a bank.
12. They are stores.
13. I am a man.
14. Centerville is a small town.
15. The Bakers' house is in New York.
16. You are a teacher.
17. I am a teacher.
18. We are teachers.
19. You are a student.
20. That is a bank.

WRITING PRACTICE

Choose one word for each space in the paragraph.

There are six people in the Baker (1)_____: Mr. Baker, Mrs. Baker and four children. The children's names are Joan, Peter, Tom and Carol. There are two boys and two (2)_____ . Peter and Tom are (3)_____ . Joan (4)_____ Carol are girls. The Bakers have a fairly large (5)_____ in Centerville. The house has six rooms. It has a living (6)_____ , a dining room, a kitchen, three bedrooms, and a bathroom.

SITUATIONAL PRACTICE

1 Ask four or five students to go to the front of the room. Find out their names. Then ask questions such as: "Who is he?", "Who is she?", "Who are they?" and let other students answer with the names.

Example: "Who is he?"   "He is Tom."
            "Who is she?"   "She is Maria."
            "Who are they?"   "They are Tom and Maria."

2 Ask each student to stand up and say, "I am _____." Then see how many names the students can remember saying; "He is Tom.", "She is Maria.", "He is Alfredo."

(*Continue.*)

3 Go to the front of the room and ask questions about the pictures in Lessons One to Four. Ask other students to answer the questions.

4 Ask questions about the things and people in the classroom. Ask the teacher or other students to answer them.

5 Ask questions about famous people. Ask other students to answer.

Example: Is _____ a man?   Yes, he is.

                      Is _____ a boy?   No, he isn't.

                      (*Continue.*)

Lesson Five

LISTENING DRILL

Step 1. Listen to your teacher pronounce the words below several times.

Step 2. Listen to your teacher say each word and decide if it is number 3, 4, 5, or 6.

Step 3. Answer with the number when the teacher pronounces the words.

3	4	5	6
pate	pet	pat	pot

READING

You remember the six people in the Baker family, don't you? There are Mr. Baker, Mrs. Baker, and four children. The children's names are Joan, Peter, Tom, and Carol. Peter and Tom are boys. Joan and Carol are girls.

Today is Monday. It is Monday afternoon. Everybody in the Baker family is busy. Mr. Baker is an auto mechanic. He is in his garage now. He is fixing a car. Mrs. Baker is a housewife. She is in the kitchen now. She is cooking dinner. Joan is a secretary. She is in the office now. She is typing a letter.

Peter, Tom, and Carol are students. They are in school now. Peter is in a classroom. He is studying Spanish. Tom is in the music room. He is playing a guitar. Carol is in the art room. She is painting a picture.

What are you doing now? What is everybody doing now? We are going to talk about that in this lesson.

"YES OR NO" QUESTIONS

Give the correct short answer, "Yes, they do", "No, they don't", etc.

1. Do Mr. and Mrs. Baker have six children?
2. Do they have four children?
3. Is Mr. Baker an auto mechanic?
4. Is he fixing a car now?
5. Is Mrs. Baker an auto mechanic?
6. Are Peter, Tom, and Carol students?
7. Is Joan a student?
8. Is Peter studying Spanish now?
9. Is Tom studying Spanish now?
10. Is Carol painting a picture now?

CONVERSATIONS

1 A. Where is Mr. Baker now?
   B. He is in the garage.
   A. What is he doing?
   B. He is fixing a car.
   A. Oh, is he an auto mechanic?
   B. Yes, he is. He is the best mechanic in Centerville.

2 A. Where is Mrs. Baker now?
   B. She's at home. She's in the kitchen.
   A. Is she washing the dishes now?
   B. No, she isn't. She's cooking dinner.
   A. Is she a good cook?
   B. Yes, she is. She's a very good cook.

3 A. Where are Peter, Tom, and Carol?
   B. They're at school now.
   A. What are they doing at school?
   B. Peter is studying Spanish now, and Tom is playing the guitar.
   A. What is Carol doing?
   B. She's painting a picture.

GRAMMAR NOTES

1. THE ALPHABET (Continued)

In Lessons Three and Four you learned the names of these 16 letters:

A B C D E F G H
I J K L M N O P

Here are five more letters. Practice repeating the names of these letters after your teacher. Remember that the name of the letter is not necessarily the same as its sound in a word:

Q R S T U

2. WHERE?

You have learned the question words *what* and *who*. *Where* is another question word. It is used to ask about the place or location of people or things.

Listen to your teacher pronounce these three question words. Then say the number that is with the word that the teacher says.

1	2	3
what	who	where

3. IN

In is a preposition. You will study more prepositions later. Prepositions often tell the location of a person or thing. They are often used in statements that answer the question "where".

Where is Peter?	He is in the classroom.
Where is the chair?	It is in the living room.
Where are the books?	They are in the classroom.

4. PRESENT CONTINUOUS VERB FORM

The present continuous verb form is usually used to talk about action taking place in the present time. It is often used with the time word *now*. The present continuous form is made with the ending *-ing* on the verb and a form of *be* (am, is, are) as an auxiliary verb. Notice these examples:

I am studying.
You are working.
Mrs. Baker is cooking.
Peter is studying Spanish.
We are speaking English.

5. PRESENT CONTINUOUS VERB FORM IN QUESTIONS

Questions are made with the present continuous by putting the auxiliary verb before the subject:

Are you studying?
Are you working?
Is Mrs. Baker cooking?
Is Peter studying Spanish?
Are we speaking English?

6. PRESENT CONTINUOUS VERB FORM IN NEGATIVE STATEMENTS

Negative statements with the present continuous verb form are made by putting *not* after the auxiliary verb. Contractions are often used in speaking:

LONG FORM	CONTRACTION
I am not cooking.	I'm not cooking.
He is not working.	He isn't working.
She is not studying.	She isn't studying.
We are not painting.	We aren't painting.
Tom is not studying Spanish.	Tom isn't studying Spanish.

7. *A* AND *THE*

The words *a* and *the* are called articles. *A* is an indefinite article. It refers to an indefinite person or thing. *The* is a definite article. It refers to a particular person or thing. The use of *a* and *the* is complicated. You will gradually learn to use them as you continue to study the language.

It is important to learn to pronounce *a* and *the* correctly. The weak, unstressed vowel sound is used with these words in most cases. The stressed vowel sound is not common when these words are used in a sentence. You should practice using only the weak, vowel sound with *a* and *the* until this has been firmly established as a habit.

The use of *a* or *the* is sometimes complicated. At times you may find it difficult to choose between them correctly. It is often impossible to translate directly from the definite and indefinite articles as they are used in your language.

As you advance in your study of English, the use of the articles will become less difficult. In the beginning it is best to follow the use given in the book or in examples given by your teacher.

39

Mr. Baker

40

Mrs. Baker

41

Joan

42

Peter

43

Tom

44

Carol

PICTURE DRILLS

1 Use the pictures from the previous lessons to review the numbers from 1 to 38.

2 Practice the numbers from 39 to 44.

39. thirty-nine	42. forty-two
40. forty	43. forty-three
41. forty-one	44. forty-four

3 Review *who* questions and answers with names.

Who is he?	He is Mr. Baker.	Who is he?	He is Peter.
Who is she?	She is Mrs. Baker.	Who is he?	He is Tom.
Who is she?	She is Joan	Who is she?	She is Carol.

4 Practice names and occupations.

Mr. Baker is a mechanic.
Mrs. Baker is a housewife.
Joan is a secretary.
Peter is a student.

Tom is a student.
Carol is a student.
Peter, Tom, and Carol are students.

5 Practice the occupations with subject pronouns.

He is a mechanic.
She is a housewife.
She is a secretary.
(*Continue.*)

He is a student.
They are students.

6 Review questions and short answers with names and occupations.

Is Mr. Baker a mechanic?   Yes, he is.
Is Mrs. Baker a mechanic?   No, she isn't.
Is Mrs. Baker a housewife?   Yes, she is.
Are Peter and Tom students?   Yes, they are.
Are Peter and Tom mechanics?   No, they aren't.
(*Continue.*)

7 Practice questions with *where.*

Where is Mr. Baker?
Where is Mrs. Baker?
Where is Joan?
(*Continue.*)

8 Practice statements with *in.*

Mr. Baker is in the garage.   Peter is in the classroom.

Mrs. Baker is in the kitchen.   Tom is in the music room.
Joan is in the office.   Carol is in the art room.
(*Continue.*)

9 Practice questions with *where* and answers with *in*.

1. Where is Mr. Baker?   He is in the garage.
2. Where is Mrs. Baker?   She is in the kitchen.
3. Where is Joan?   She is in the office.
   (*Continue.*)

10 Practice questions with *what* and the present continuous verb form.

1. What is Mr. Baker doing?
2. What is Mrs. Baker doing?
3. What is Joan doing?
   (*Continue.*)

11 Practice statements with the present continuous verb form.

1. Mr. Baker is fixing a car.   4. Peter is studying Spanish.
2. Mrs. Baker is cooking dinner.   5. Tom is playing a guitar.
3. Joan is typing a letter.   6. Carol is painting a picture.

12 Practice questions and answers with the present continuous verb form.

1. What is Mr. Baker doing?   He is fixing a car.
2. What is Mrs. Baker doing?   She is cooking dinner.
3. What is Joan doing?   She is typing a letter.

13 Summary Drill. Practice a series of related questions and answers.

1. Who is he?   He is Mr. Baker.
2. Where is he?   He is in the garage.
3. What is he doing?   He is fixing a car.
4. Is he a mechanic?   Yes, he is.
5. What is that?   It is a car.
   (*Continue.*)

SUBSTITUTION DRILLS

1 Review the days of the week. Follow the example.

Example: Monday   *Today is Monday.*

1. Monday   5. Friday
2. Tuesday   6. Saturday
3. Wednesday   7. Sunday
4. Thursday

2 Review the numbers from one to twenty-four. Follow the example.

Example: three   *This is number three.*

1. one	9. nine	17. seventeen
2. two	10. ten	18. eighteen
3. three	11. eleven	19. nineteen
4. four	12. twelve	20. twenty
5. five	13. thirteen	21. twenty-one
6. six	14. fourteen	22. twenty-two
7. seven	15. fifteen	23. twenty-three
8. eight	16. sixteen	24. twenty-four

3 Practice questions with *where*. Follow the examples.

Examples: he   *Where is he?*
            they *Where are they?*

1. he	9. that town
2. she	10. the school
3. you	11. the house
4. that man	12. you
5. they	13. he
6. those boys	14. Peter
7. the book	15. Peter and Tom
8. the books	16. the children

4 Practice statements with *in*. Follow the example.

Example: Mrs. Baker/the kitchen
              Mrs. Baker is in the kitchen.

1. Mr. Baker/the garage	8. they/the bedroom
2. Joan/the office	9. Carol/the art room
3. Mrs. Baker/the kitchen	10. we/school
4. Peter and Tom/school	11. you/school
5. I/the classroom	12. the Bakers/the house
6. we/the classroom	13. he/the bathroom
7. he/the living room	14. they/the dining room

5 Practice questions with *what* and the present continuous verb *doing*. Follow the examples.

Examples: he   *What is he doing now?*
            they *What are they doing now?*

1. she	7. Mr. and Mrs. Baker
2. they	8. those girls
3. we	9. you
4. Peter	10. I
5. Tom	11. he
6. Peter and Tom	12. the boys

6 Practice statements with *now* and the present continuous verb form. Follow the example.

Example: he/fix the car   *He is fixing the car now.*

1. she/cook
2. I/study
3. we/study
4. we/study English
5. Tom/play the guitar
6. Peter/study Spanish
7. she/paint
8. she/paint a picture
9. Peter and Tom/study
10. they/study
11. I/speak English
12. we/speak English
13. you/speak English
14. Joan/type
15. Joan/type a letter
16. we/practice English

7 Practice questions with *now* and the present continuous verb form. Follow the example.

Example: they/study   *Are they studying now?*

1. you/study
2. she/cook
3. she/cook dinner
4. they/eat dinner
5. Mr. Baker/fix a car
6. we/speak Spanish
7. I/speak good English
8. those boys/listen
9. he/work
10. Joan/type a letter
11. Peter/study Spanish
12. Tom/play the guitar
13. Carol/paint a picture
14. Tom/study English
15. you/read
16. you/listen

8 Practice negative statements with *now* and the present continuous verb form. Follow the example.

Example: Mrs. Baker/fix the car
Mrs. Baker isn't fixing the car now.

1. I/study Spanish
2. we/speak Spanish
3. Mr. Baker/cook dinner
4. Peter/wash the dishes
5. Tom/study English
6. we/sleep
7. they/eat
8. you/paint the room
9. you/speak Spanish
10. Joan/study
11. I/eat dinner
12. we/play
13. you/sleep
14. I/wash the dishes
15. Joan/fix the car
16. we/listen

TRANSFORMATION DRILLS

1 Change from singular to plural. Follow the example.

Example: Singular   This is a book.
Plural   *These are books.*

1. This is a school.
2. That is a knife.
3. This is a store.
4. That is a pencil.
5. This is a car.
6. It is a pen.

7. This is a plate.   10. It is a garage.
8. That is a table.   11. It is a classroom.
9. That is a chair.   12. It is a guitar.

2 Change from statements to questions. Follow the example.

Example:	Statement	He is studying.
	Question	*Is he studying?*

1. He is playing the guitar now.
2. She is typing.
3. She is in the office.
4. They are in school.
5. Mrs. Baker is in the kitchen
6. She is a housewife.
7. She is cooking dinner now.
8. She is a woman.
9. They are women.
10. Tom is a boy.
11. Peter and Tom are boys.
12. Carol is a student.
13. Peter, Tom, and Carol are students.

14. He is an auto mechanic.
15. Joan is a secretary.
16. They are men.
17. This is a chair.
18. That is a table.
19. Those are spoons.
20. Those are plates.
21. It is a house.
22. The Bakers are in the house.
23. Mrs. Baker is cooking dinner.
24. They are eating dinner.
25. Peter and Tom are watching TV now.

3 Change the names to subject pronouns. Follow the example.

Example:	Name	Tom is a boy.
	Subject Pronoun	*He is a boy.*

1. Peter is a boy.
2. Carol is a girl.
3. Peter and Tom are boys.
4. Mrs. Baker is a woman.
5. Mr. Baker is a man.
6. Mrs. Baker and Mrs. Hill are women.
7. Mr. Baker and Mr. Hill are men.
8. Peter and Tom are students.
9. Peter, Tom, and Carol are students in that school.

10. Joan is a secretary.
11. Joan is in the office now.
12. Joan is typing a letter now.
13. Mrs. Baker is a housewife.
14. Mrs. Hill is a housewife, too.
15. Mrs. Baker and Mrs. Hill are in the kitchen now.
16. Mr. Baker is a mechanic.
17. Mr. Baker is fixing a car now.
18. Carol is painting a picture now.

4 Change from affirmative to negative. Follow the example.

Example:	Affirmative	Tom is in the kitchen.
	Negative	*Tom isn't in the kitchen.*

1. Tom is cooking dinner.
2. Peter is typing a letter now.
3. They are fixing the car now.
4. The car is in the bathroom.
5. Joan is in the living room now.
6. Mr. Baker is in the bathroom.
7. This is a large book.

8. You are a secretary.
9. Mr. Baker is a boy.
10. Peter is in the art room.
11. Tom is playing the guitar in the bathroom.
12. The TV set is in the refrigerator.
13. I am studying auto mechanics.
14. We are studying Japanese now.

15. These are cups.
16. I am a mechanic
17. We are speaking Spanish now.
18. We are speaking Chinese now.

19. Mr. Hill is an auto mechanic.
20. Centerville is a small town in England.
21. The Bakers' house is in New York City.
22. This is a question.

WRITING PRACTICE

Choose one word for each space in the paragraph.

Today is Monday. It (1)_____ Monday afternoon. Everybody in the Baker family is busy. Mrs. (2)_____ is an auto mechanic. He is in his garage now. He is fixing a (3) _____ . Mrs. Baker is a housewife. (4)_____ is in the kitchen now. She is cooking dinner. Joan is a secretary. She is (5)_____ the office now. She is typing a letter. Peter, Tom, and Carol (6)_____ students. They are in (7)_____ now. Peter is in a classroom. He is studying Spanish. Tom is in the music room. He is (8)_____ a guitar. Carol is in the art room. She is painting a picture.

SITUATIONAL PRACTICE

1 Go to the front of the room and count the picture cards out loud. Then ask other students "What number is this?" The students answer: "It is number_____."

2 Ask questions about the picture cards. Let other students answer. Use the various questions that you have practiced in Lessons One to Five.

3 Ask questions about the things and people in the room. Let other students answer. Use the various question patterns that you have practiced in Lessons One to Five. Be sure to use the question words *who*, *what* and *where*.

4 If you have learned the vocabulary for Lesson Five, you can learn some more verbs by practicing action games. Perform an action, and then ask a student what you are doing.

Example: Student A: (Picks up book and starts to read.)
                          "What am I doing?"
            Student B: "You are reading."

Here are some other verbs that you can play this game with:

walk   dance
sit   sing
write   run
open (the door, window, book)   close (the door, window, book)

5 Play "True or False" with actions. Perform an action and make a statement. Ask students to tell whether the statement is true or false.

Lesson Six

People in Centerville

Step 1. Listen to your teacher pronounce the words below several times.

Step 2. Listen to your teacher say each word and decide if it is number 4, 5, 6, or 7.

Step 3. Answer with the number when the teacher pronounces the words.

4	5	6	7
den	Dan	Don	dawn

READING

You remember Centerville, don't you? The Bakers live in Centerville. Mr. Baker is an auto mechanic. Mrs. Baker is a housewife. They have four children. Joan is a secretary. Peter, Tom, and Carol are students.

Many other people live in Centerville, too. Some of the people are rich and some are poor. Some are young and some are old. Some are tall and some are short. Some of the people are happy and some are sad. There are people of many different races and religions.

In this lesson we are going to talk about some of the people in Centerville. We are going to talk about two men, two women, two boys, and two girls. Their names are: Mr. Smith, Mr. Kent, Mrs. Clark, Mrs. Hill, Jerry, Don, Mary, and Sharon. Mr. Smith and Mr. Kent are men. Mrs. Clark and Mrs. Hill are women. Jerry and Don are boys. Mary and Sharon are girls. Mr. Smith is rich, but Mr. Kent is poor. Mrs. Clark is old. Mrs. Hill is young. Jerry is tall. Don is short. Mary is a big girl. Sharon is small.

"YES OR NO" QUESTIONS

Give the correct short answer.

1. Do the Bakers live in Centerville?
2. Do many other people live in Centerville, too?
3. Is Mr. Smith a man?
4. Are Jerry and Don men?
5. Are they boys?
6. Are Mrs. Clark and Mrs. Hill women?

"OR" QUESTIONS

Give the correct short answer.

1. Is Mr. Smith rich or poor?
2. Is Mrs. Clark young or old?
3. Is Jerry tall or short?
4. Is Sharon large or small?

CONVERSATIONS

1   A. Jerry is a tall boy, isn't he?
    B. Yes, he is. He's very tall.
    A. What is he doing now?
    B. He's singing.
    A. Where is he singing?
    B. He's singing in the church.

2   A. Who are those girls?
    B. They are Mary and Sharon.
    A. Which girl is Mary, and which is Sharon?
    B. Mary is a big girl. Sharon is small.
    A. Oh, yes. Mary is reading now, isn't she?
    B. Yes, she is, and Sharon is writing.

3   A. What are you doing now?
    B. I'm studying.
    A. What are you studying?
    B. I'm studying English.
    A. English is difficult, isn't it?
    B. Sometimes it's difficult. Sometimes it's easy.
    A. Where are you studying?
    B. I'm studying at school. The classes are very good.

GRAMMAR NOTES

1. THE ALPHABET (Continued)

There are 26 letters in the English alphabet. You have learned the names of 21 of them:

A   B   C   D   E   F   G   H   I   J
K   L   M   N   O   P   Q   R   S   T   U

Here are the last five letters:

V   W   X   Y   Z

Practice repeating the names of all the letters after your teacher. Learn how to spell your name out loud.

Remember that the name of a letter is often very different than its sound in a word and that some letters have different sounds in different words.

2. A AND *AN*

A and *an* are two forms of one word. Before a vowel sound we use *an*. Before a consonant sound we use *a*. Notice these examples:

BEFORE A VOWEL SOUND	*BEFORE A CONSONANT SOUND*
an orange	a house
an egg	a book
an elephant	a table
an old man	a young man

3. ADJECTIVES

In this lesson we practice with a group of words called *adjectives*. Adjectives usually describe or modify nouns. In English, adjectives do not change form for person or number. They do not change for gender, either. Some adjectives change form for comparative or superlative expressions. You will study these later. Here are adjectives that you will practice in this lesson:

difficult	easy
big	small
tall	short
young	old
good	bad
happy	sad
rich	poor

Big and *large* have almost the same meaning. *Young* and *new* have similar meanings. *Young* is usually used for people and other living things. *New* is usually used for non-living things.

4. POSITION OF ADJECTIVES

English adjectives often appear in the predicate after a form of the linking verb *be* (*am*, *is*, *are*):

I am young.	This book is old.
You are tall.	Mr. Smith is rich.
He is happy.	Centerville is large.

Adjectives also often come before nouns:

The tall boy is singing.	The old man is eating.
These are good books.	Peter is a good student.
He is an old man.	I am a good student.

5. WHICH

You have learned three question words so far: *who*, *what*, and *where*. *Which* is another question word. *Which* is usually used to ask about one out of a group of two or more things.

Listen to your teacher pronounce these four question words, see if you can identify the word that the teacher says by giving its number, and then repeat the words after your teacher:

1	2	3	4
who	what	where	which

Here are some examples to help you understand the meaning and use of *which*:

Which man is Mr. Smith?	The rich man is Mr. Smith.
Which house is the Bakers'?	That house is the Bakers'.
Which book are you reading?	I am reading the English book.

6. PEOPLE

People has a plural sense. It is used with the verb *are* and other plural forms. There is no singular form for this word. For the singular, *person* or some similar word is used.

SINGULAR	PLURAL
He is a person.	They are people.
I am a good person.	We are good people.

There is a form of *people* with an "s" ending - *peoples.* This is used to refer to groups or categories of people.

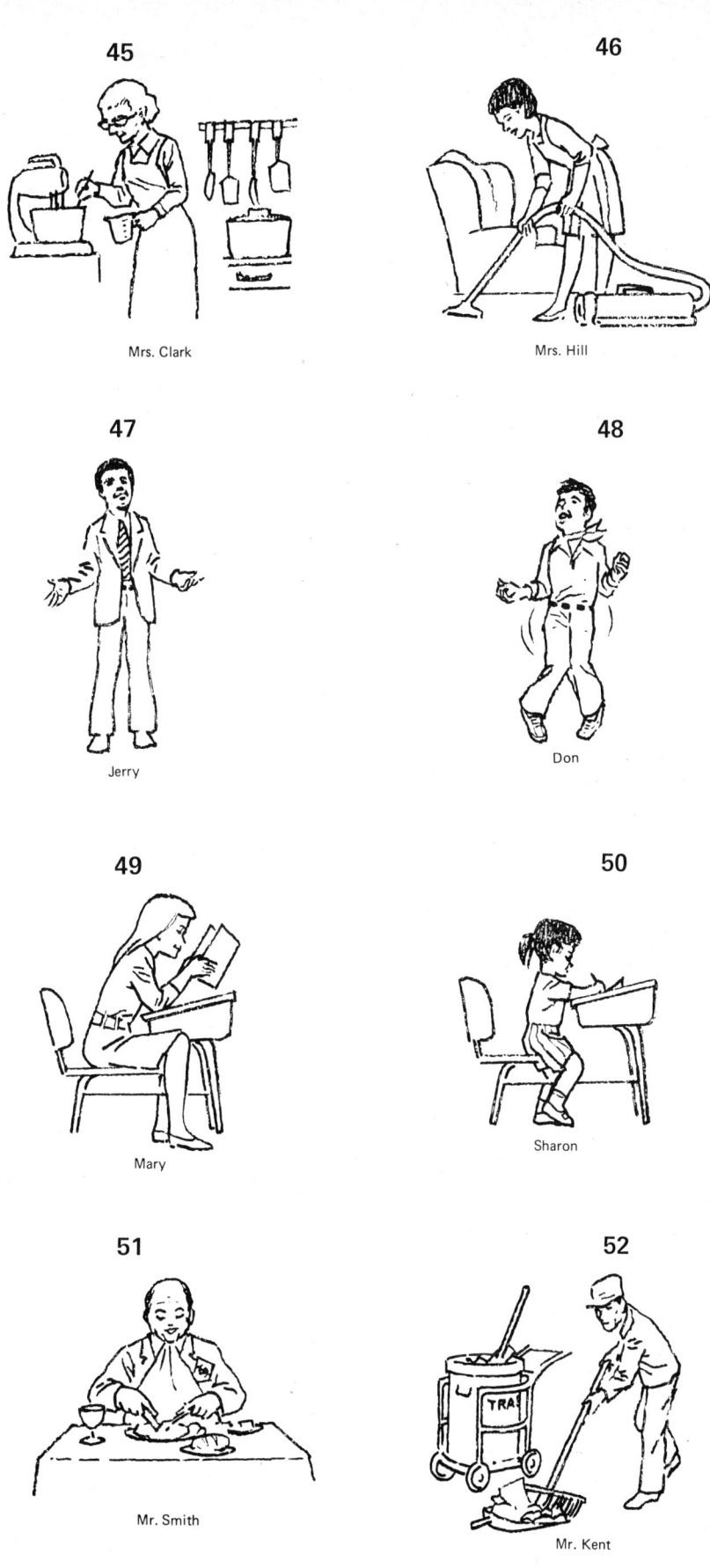

45

Mrs. Clark

46

Mrs. Hill

47

Jerry

48

Don

49

Mary

50

Sharon

51

Mr. Smith

52

Mr. Kent

PICTURE DRILLS

1 Review the numbers from 1 to 44.

2 Practice the numbers from 45 to 52.

45. forty-five	49. forty-nine
46. forty-six	50. fifty
47. forty-seven	51. fifty-one
48. forty-eight	52. fifty-two

3 Practice the names of the people in the pictures.

1. Mrs. Clark	5. Mary
2. Mrs. Hill	6. Sharon
3. Jerry	7. Mr. Smith
4. Don	8. Mr. Kent

4 Practice the names in statements.

1. Mrs. Clark is a woman.	5. Mary is a girl.
2. Mrs. Hill is a woman.	6. Sharon is a girl.
3. Jerry is a boy.	7. Mr. Smith is a man.
4. Don is a boy.	8. Mr. Kent is a man.

5 Review plural forms with the names.

1. Mrs. Clark and Mrs. Hill are women.
2. Jerry and Don are boys.
3. Mary and Sharon are girls.
4. Mr. Smith and Mr. Kent are men.

6 Practice the names with predicate adjectives.

1. Mrs. Clark is old.	5. Mary is big.
2. Mrs. Hill is young.	6. Sharon is small.
3. Jerry is tall.	7. Mr. Smith is rich.
4. Don is short.	8. Mr. Kent is poor.

7 Practice the position of adjectives before nouns.

Mrs. Clark is a woman.
Mrs. Clark is old.   Mrs. Clark is an old woman.

Jerry is a boy.
Jerry is tall.   Jerry is a tall boy.

Mary is big.
Mary is a girl.   Mary is a big girl.
(*Continue.*)

8 Practice question patterns with adjectives.

1. Is Mrs. Clark an old woman?	Yes, she is.
2. Is Mrs. Hill an old woman?	No, she isn't.
3. Is Jerry a tall boy?	Yes, he is.
4. Is Don a tall boy?	No, he isn't.
5. Is Don a short boy?	Yes, he is.
(*Continue.*)	

9 Review the present continuous verb form in questions with *what*.

1. What is Mrs. Clark doing?
2. What is Mrs. Hill doing?
3. What is Jerry doing?
   (*Continue.*)

10 Practice present continuous verb forms with the names. Use the time word *now*.

1. Mrs. Clark is cooking now.	5. Mary is reading now.
2. Mrs. Hill is cleaning now.	6. Sharon is writing now.
3. Jerry is singing now.	7. Mr. Smith is eating now.
4. Don is dancing now.	8. Mr. Kent is working now.

11 Practice questions with adjectives and answers with subject pronouns.

(The pictures should be displayed as a group on the wall in order to force a choice determined by the adjective in the question.)

1. What is the old woman doing now?	She is cooking.
2. What is the young woman doing now?	She is cleaning.
3. What is the short boy doing now?	He is dancing.
4. What is the tall boy doing now?	He is singing.
5. What is the poor man doing now?	He is working.
6. What is the small girl doing now?	She is writing.
(*Continue.*)	

12 Practice questions with *which*.

1. Which woman is cooking?
2. Which woman is cleaning?
3. Which boy is singing?
4. Which boy is dancing?
   (*Continue.*)

13 Practice questions with *which* and answers with names.

1. Which woman is cooking?	Mrs. Clark is cooking.
2. Which woman is cleaning?	Mrs. Hill is cleaning.
3. Which boy is dancing?	Don is dancing.
4. Which girl is reading?	Mary is reading.
(*Continue.*)	

14 Practice questions with *which* and answers with adjectives.

(The names on the picture cards should be covered with strips of paper or by some other means for this drill.)

1. Which woman is cooking?   The old woman is cooking.
2. Which woman is cleaning?   The young woman is cleaning.
3. Which boy is dancing?   The short boy is dancing.
4. Which girl is writing?   The small girl is writing.
   (Continue.)

15 Summary Drill.   Practice various question-and-answer patterns that have been drilled in Lessons One to Six.

1. What is this?   It is a stove.
2. Who is she?   She is Mrs. Clark.
3. What is she doing?   She is cooking.
4. Is she a woman?   Yes, she is.
5. Is she a young woman?   No, she isn't.
6. Is she an old woman?   Yes, she is.
7. Where is she cooking?   She is cooking in the kitchen.
8. What is she cooking?   She is cooking dinner.
9. Who is that boy?   That is Jerry.
10. What is he doing?   He is singing.
11. Is he a tall boy?   Yes, he is.
    (Continue.)

SUBSTITUTION DRILLS

1 Practice statements with predicate adjectives.

Example: he/tall   *He is tall.*

1. She/young   7. Peter and Tom/happy
2. Carol/young   8. that girl/tall
3. Peter/tall   9. those girls/happy
4. he/tall   10. Mrs. Clark/old
5. they/rich   11. Mrs. Hill/young
6. I/happy   12. this book/good

2 Practice statements with predicate nouns.

Example: he/a man   *He is a man.*

1. she/a woman   7. she/a housewife
2. he/a man   8. this/a school
3. they/men   9. those/houses
4. this/a shirt   10. Mr. Smith/a man
5. you/a teacher   11. I/a student
6. Mr. Baker/a mechanic 12. we/students

3 Practice statements with predicate adjectives before predicate nouns.

Example: he/a tall boy   *He is a tall boy.*

1. he/a short boy
2. she/ a big girl
3. she/an old woman
4. they/old men
5. we/good students
6. I/a good student
7. this/a small hat
8. these/small hats
9. he/a young boy
10. those/big shoes
11. it/a big school
12. they/big schools

4 Practice statements with adjectives before the subject noun. Use the present continuous verb form. Use the time word *now*.

Examples: tall boy/sing   *The tall boy is singing now.*
old woman/cook   *The old woman is cooking now.*

1. young woman/clean
2. old woman/cook
3. rich man/eat
4. rich man/eat/dinner
5. tall boy/study
6. tall boy/study/English
7. small girl/paint
8. small girl/paint a picture
9. young man/work
10. young man/work in the bank
11. old man/eat
12. old man/eat/in the dining room
13. young girl/read
14. young girl/read/in the bedroom
15. young woman/work in the store
16. young women/work in the store

TRANSFORMATION DRILLS

1 Make one sentence by combining the two sentences given.

Example: He is young.
+ He is a man.   *He is a young man.*

1. She is small.
   She is a girl.
2. She is a woman.
   She is big.
3. I am good.
   I am a student.
4. They are tall.
   They are boys.
5. We are young.
   We are people.
6. He is a man.
   He is good.
7. They are bad.
   They are boys.
8. Peter is a student.
   Peter is good.
9. Joan is good.
   Joan is a secretary.
10. Mr. Smith is rich.
    Mr. Smith is a man.
11. You are a teacher.
    You are good.
12. We are good.
    We are English students.
13. Mr. and Mrs. Baker are good.
    Mr. and Mrs. Baker are people.
14. I am good.
    I am a person.
15. English is a language.
    English is difficult.

2 Change from singular to plural. Notice that there is no plural form of the adjective.

Example: Singular   This is a good book.
            Plural   *These are good books.*

1. This is a small house.
2. That is a big store.
3. He is a young boy.
4. The man is working.
5. The young man is working.
6. The student is studying.
7. The good student is studying.
8. That school is good.
9. That hat is old.
10. This drill is difficult.
11. I am a good student.
12. This is a good class.
13. He is a bad boy.
14. The bad boy isn't studying.
15. The poor man isn't eating.

3 Change these statements to questions.

Example: Statement   The old man is eating.
            Question   *Is the old man eating?*

1. She is a girl.
2. I am a good student.
3. English is difficult.
4. We are studying English.
5. The boys are working in the garage now.
6. Mr. Baker is fixing that old car.
7. Mrs. Baker is cooking a good dinner.
8. We are speaking good English now.
9. That old man is eating dinner in the dining room now.
10. You are speaking English now.
11. That is an old house.
12. Mr. Smith is a rich man.
13. They are living in a big old house.
14. This is an easy English book.
15. We are doing easy drills.
16. We are changing these sentences from statements to questions.
17. I am studying English in this class.
18. The teacher is a good person.
19. Centerville is a large town.
20. Centerville is a large town in the United States.

WRITING PRACTICE

Choose one word for each space in the paragraph.

The Bakers (1) _____ in Centerville. Mr. Baker (2)_____ an auto mechanic. Mrs. Baker is a housewife. They have four (3)_____ . Joan is a secretary. Peter, Tom, and Carol (4)_____ students. Many other people live (5)_____ Centerville, too. Some of the (6)_____ are rich and some are poor. Some are young (7)_____ some are old. Some are tall and some are (8)_____ . Some of the people are happy and some (9)_____ sad.

SITUATIONAL PRACTICE

1 Play "questions and answers" with the picture cards from Lesson Six.

2 Play "questions and answers" with the picture cards from Lessons One to Five.

3 Make statements about things in the room using the adjectives from Lesson Six.

Examples: "This is a big desk."
              "These are old books."
              "That is a short pencil."
              (*Continue.*)

If you have learned all the adjectives given in Lesson Six, your teacher may give you additional ones such as *wide, narrow, long*, etc.

4 Review the "action game" using verbs in the present continuous form. Perform an action and ask, "What am I doing now?" Ask students to answer with a present continuous verb form.

Example: "You are reading."

5 Ask two students to come to the front of the room and perform two different actions. Then ask, for example, "Which student is walking?" Have other students answer using names, "José is walking." or adjectives, "The tall boy is walking."

6 Practice making questions with *where* and answers with the prepositions *in* and *on*. For example, place a short pencil on a desk and a long pencil on a chair and ask, "Where is the long pencil?" Students will answer, "It is on a chair." Ask, "Where is the short pencil?" and students answer, "It is on the desk." You can work out other variations of this game using other objects or using students.

Lesson Seven

Peter's Friends

LISTENING DRILL

Step 1. Listen to your teacher pronounce the words below several times.
Step 2. Listen to your teacher say each word and decide if it is number 5, 6, 7, or 8.
Step 3. Answer with the number when the teacher pronounces the words.

5	6	7	8
cad	cod	cawed	code

READING

Do you remember the tall boy singing in the church? He is Jerry Hill. Peter Baker and Jerry Hill are good friends. Peter often visits Jerry's house. Everybody in the Hill family likes Peter. They are all Peter's friends.

Jerry's father is Mr. Hill. Mr. Hill is a postman. He is forty-one years old. He is a big, strong man. Jerry's mother is Mrs. Hill. She is thirty-six years old. She is a good wife and a good mother. Jerry has one sister. Her name is Linda. Linda is fourteen years old. She is a pretty young girl.

Mrs. Hill has a sister named Mrs. Carter. Mrs. Carter's husband is dead. He died in the war. Mrs. Carter is thirty-two years old. She is a teacher in the Centerville High School. Mrs. Carter has a daughter named Sharon. Sharon is five years old. She is just a little girl. Mrs. Carter and Sharon live with the Hills.

In this lesson we are going to talk about the Hill family. We are going to talk about Mr. Hill, Mrs. Hill, Jerry, Linda, Mrs. Carter, and Sharon. We are going to practice with "family words" such as "father", "mother", "sister", "brother", and so on.

"YES OR NO" QUESTIONS

Give the correct short answer.

1. Are Peter and Jerry good friends?
2. Is Jerry's father an auto mechanic?
3. Is he a postman?
4. Is Mrs. Hill thirty-six years old?
5. Is Mrs. Hill an old woman?
6. Do the Hills live in Centerville?
7. Does Mrs. Carter teach in the Centerville High School?
8. Is Mrs. Carter's husband dead?

"OR" QUESTIONS

1. Is Jerry a tall boy or a short boy?
2. Is Mr. Hill a postman or an auto mechanic?
3. Is Mrs. Hill a young woman or an old woman?
4. Do the Hills live in New York or in Centerville?
5. Is Sharon a big girl or a little girl?
6. Is Mrs. Carter a housewife or a teacher?

CONVERSATIONS

1   A. Who is that boy?
    B. That's Jerry Hill.
    A. Oh! Is he Peter's friend?
    B. Yes, he is. Jerry and Peter are good friends.
    A. How old is Jerry?
    B. He's about seventeen years old.

2   A. Mrs. Hill is Jerry's mother, isn't she?
    B. Yes, she is.
    A. Who is Mrs. Carter?
    B. Mrs. Carter is Mrs. Hill's sister.
    A. Oh, I see. Mrs. Carter is Jerry's aunt, isn't she?
    B. Yes, that's right.

3   A. What is Jerry's father doing now?
    B. He is working.
    A. Where is he working?
    B. He is working in the Post Office.
    A. He is a strong man, isn't he?
    B. Yes, he is. He's very strong and healthy.

GRAMMAR NOTES

1. AGE

English uses forms of the linking verb *be* to talk about age. Here are some examples:

How old *is* he?   He *is* fifteen years old.   How old *are* Jerry and Peter?
How old *are* you?   I *am* twenty years old.   Tom *is* twelve years old.
How old *is* Jerry?   Jerry *is* seventeen years old.   The baby *is* one year old.

Sometimes we do not use the expression *years old:*

He is fifteen.
I am twenty.
Jerry is seventeen.

2. POSSESSIVE NOUNS

When a person has or owns something we say he *possesses* it. To express possession in English we often use possessive nouns. We make possessive nouns by adding *'s* at the end of the noun. Notice these examples:

NOUN (SINGULAR)	*POSSESSIVE FORM*
Jerry	Jerry's
Linda	Linda's
Peter	Peter's
the school	the school's
the student	the student's
the teacher	the teacher's

When the noun is plural and ends in *s* we just add the apostrophe (') after that *s*. Notice these examples:

PLURAL NOUN	POSSESSIVE FORM
the boys	the boys'
the girls	the girls'
two students	two students'
the Hills	the Hills'
the Bakers	the Bakers'

3. FAMILY MEMBERS

In this lesson we practice with the words for family relationships. Here are the most common of these words in English:

MALE	FEMALE
father	mother
husband	wife
son	daughter
brother	sister
uncle	aunt
grandfather	grandmother
grandson	granddaughter
nephew	niece

When the relationship is a result of marriage, we use the expression, *-in-law*. Here are the most common of these:

father-in-law	mother-in-law
son-in-law	daughter-in-law
brother-in-law	sister-in-law

Cousin is used for both male and female relatives.

4. ADJECTIVES (Continued)

In this lesson we practice with these five new adjectives:

strong
handsome
pretty
intelligent
little

Remember that English adjectives come before the noun that they modify:

He is a strong man.	She is an intelligent teacher.
Jerry is a handsome boy.	This is a little house.
Mrs. Hill is a pretty woman.	The small girl is Sharon.

53

54

55

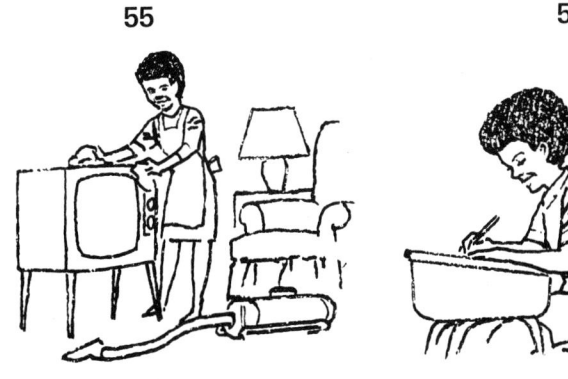

56

57

58

PICTURE DRILLS

1 Review the numbers from 1 to 52 using the pictures from previous lessons.

2 Practice the numbers from 53 to 58.

53. fifty-three	56. fifty-six
54. fifty-four	57. fifty-seven
55. fifty-five	58. fifty-eight

3 Practice the names of the people in the pictures.

1. Mr. Hill	4. Linda Hill
2. Jerry Hill	5. Mrs. Carter
3. Mrs. Hill	6. Sharon Carter

4 Practice questions about age.

1. How old is Mr. Hill?
2. How old is Jerry Hill?
3. How old is Mrs. Hill?
   (*Continue.*)

5 Practice statements about age.

1. Mr. Hill is forty-one years old.	4. Linda Hill is fourteen years old.
2. Jerry is seventeen years old.	5. Mrs. Carter is thirty-two years old.
3. Mrs. Hill is thirty-six years old.	6. Sharon Carter is five years old.

6 Practice the present continuous verb form in statements.

1. Mr. Hill is working now.	4. Linda is writing now.
2. Jerry is swimming now.	5. Mrs. Carter is teaching now.
3. Mrs. Hill is cleaning now.	6. Sharon is sleeping now.

7 Practice questions with possessive nouns and words for family relationships.

(*For this drill all the pictures except the one of Jerry should be placed on the wall or tack board. Hold the picture of Jerry in your hand.*)

1. What is Jerry's father doing now?	He is working.
2. What is Jerry's mother doing now?	She is cleaning.
3. What is Jerry's sister doing now?	She is writing.
4. What is Jerry's aunt doing now?	She is teaching.
5. What is Jerry's cousin doing now?	She is sleeping.

Note.   This drill may be varied and repeated many times by separating a different person's picture from the group and asking questions with different family words. For example:

1. What is Mr. Hill's wife doing?
2. What is Mr. Hill's son doing?
   (*Continue.*)

1. What is Mrs. Hill's husband doing?
2. What is Mrs. Hill's sister doing?
   (*Continue.*)

8 Practice questions with *where* using possessive nouns and words for family relationships.

(*Separate Linda's picture from the group.*)

1. Where is Linda's father working now?
   He is working in the Post Office.

2. Where is Linda's brother swimming now?
   He is swimming in the pool.

3. Where is Linda's mother cleaning now?
   She is cleaning in the living room.

4. Where is Linda's aunt teaching now?
   She is teaching in the high school.

5. Where is Linda's cousin sleeping now?
   She is sleeping in the bedroom.

Note.   As in drill 7, this drill may be repeated many times by separating a different person's picture from the group.

9 Practice "yes or no" questions with possessive nouns and words for family relationships. Give short answers.

1. Is Jerry's mother cleaning now?   Yes, she is.
2. Is Jerry's father sleeping now?   No, he isn't.
3. Is Linda's brother swimming now?   Yes, he is.
4. Is Mrs. Carter's daughter sleeping now? Yes, she is.
5. Is Mr. Hill's wife eating now?   No, she isn't.
   (*Continue.*)

10 Practice statements with predicate adjectives.

1. Mr. Hill is strong.   4. Linda is pretty.
2. Jerry is handsome.   5. Mrs. Carter is intelligent.
3. Mrs. Hill is young.   6. Sharon is little.

11 Practice statements with adjectives before nouns.

1. Mr. Hill is a strong man.   4. Linda is a pretty girl.
2. Jerry is a handsome boy.   5. Mrs. Carter is an intelligent woman.
3. Mrs. Hill is a young woman.   6. Sharon is a little girl.

12 Practice statements with possessive nouns, words for family relationships, and adjectives.

(First indicate Mrs. Hill's picture.)

1. Mrs. Hill's husband is a strong man.
2. Mrs. Hill's son is a handsome boy.
3. Mrs. Hill's daughter is a pretty girl.
   (Continue.)

Note. As in drills 7 and 8, this drill should be repeated several times with different persons' pictures separated from the group.

13 Summary Drill. Practice various questions and answers with the pictures.

1. Who is he?	He is Mr. Hill.
2. How old is he?	He is forty-one years old.
3. What is Mr. Hill's son doing now?	He is swimming.
4. Is Mr. Hill's wife swimming, too?	No, she isn't.
5. Is Mr. Hill a strong man?	Yes, he is.
6. What is Mr. Hill doing now?	He is working.
7. Where is he working?	In the Post Office.
8. Is he a postman?	Yes, he is.
(Continue.)	

SUBSTITUTION DRILLS

1 Review the names of the letters of the alphabet.

```
A  B  C  D  E  F  G  H  I
J  K  L  M  N  O  P  Q  R
S  T  U  V  W  X  Y  Z
```

2 Review the days of the week.

Example: Sunday *Today is Sunday.*

1. Sunday
2. Monday
3. Tuesday
4. Wednesday
5. Thursday
6. Friday
7. Saturday

3 Practice the possessive form of nouns. Give the possessive form of the singular nouns given.

Example: Jerry *Jerry's*

1. Jerry
2. Mr. Hill
3. Peter
4. Linda
5. Tom
6. Joan
7. Carol
8. Mrs. Hill
9. Mrs. Carter
10. Sharon

4 Practice using possessive nouns in sentences.

Example: Jerry/father/strong   *Jerry's father is strong.*

1. Jerry/mother/young
2. Peter/brother/short
3. Mr. Baker/daughter/pretty
4. Sharon/cousins/good students
5. Tom/sister/in the art room
6. Jerry/books/in the classroom
7. Peter/friends/in the pool
8. Joan/brothers/Peter and Tom
9. Mr. Hill/wife/cleaning
   in the living room
10. Mrs. Baker/husband/fixing a car
    in the garage now
11. Mrs. Carter/daughter/sleeping
    in the bedroom now
12. Mrs. Carter/husband/dead
13. Carol/shoes/in the bedroom
14. Peter/pencil/in the desk
15. Mr. Hill/children/students
16. Mrs. Hill/husband/postman

TRANSFORMATION DRILLS

1 Make one sentence by combining the two sentences given.

Example: Jerry's father is a man.
         + Jerry's father is strong.   *Jerry's father is a strong man.*

1. Jerry's mother is a woman.
   Jerry's mother is young.

2. Jerry's friend is a boy.
   Jerry's friend is short.

3. Linda's cousin is a girl.
   Linda's cousin is little.

4. Peter's brother is a boy.
   Peter's brother is short.

5. Mr. Smith's father is a man.
   Mr. Smith's father is very old.

6. Mrs. Carter's students are boys and girls.
   Mrs. Carter's students are intelligent.

7. This is a drill.
   This is difficult.

8. English is a language.
   English is difficult.

9. He is a man.
   He is handsome.

10. Peter's sister is a girl.
    Peter's sister is pretty.

11. We are students.
    We are good.

12. I am a person.
    I am good.

13. Mr. Hill's wife is a woman.
    Mr. Hill's wife is young.

2 Change these statements to questions.

Example: Statement Jerry's sister is a pretty girl.
         Question *Is Jerry's sister a pretty girl?*

1. Mrs. Hill's son is swimming now.
2. Mr. Hill's wife is cleaning now.
3. Jerry's father is a strong man. ·
4. Sharon's cousins are good students.
5. This is an easy lesson.
6. Peter is a tall boy.
7. Jerry's house is near the school.
8. Peter's sister is a secretary.
9. Peter's mother is a housewife.
10. These are small cups.
11. Those boys are studying English now.
12. She is sad today.

13. You are speaking English now.
14. That is a difficult book.
15. I am an intelligent student.
16. Mr. Baker is a mechanic.
17. Peter and Jerry are good friends.

18. Today is Wednesday.
19. She is cooking dinner in the kitchen.
20. Jerry's father is working in the Post Office.

WRITING PRACTICE

Choose one word for each space in the paragraph.

Do you remember the tall boy singing in the church? He (1)_____ Jerry Hill. Jerry's (2)_____ is Mr. Hill. Mr Hill is a postman. He (3)_____ forty-one years old. He is a big, strong (4)_____. Jerry's mother is (5)_____ Hill. She is thirty-six. (6)_____ old. She is a good wife and a good (7)_____. Jerry has one sister. Her name is Linda. Linda is fourteen (8)_____ old. She is a pretty young girl.

SITUATIONAL PRACTICE

1 Find out the age of your classmates.

Example: A: "How old are you?"
              B: "*I am _____ years old.*"

2 Find out who can remember the age of your classmates.

Example: A: "How old is _____?"
              B: "_____ *is* _____ years old."

3 Practice the possessive form of the names of all the students in the class. You can also practice using the possessive form of their names with something that the student owns.

Example: Tom's pencil
              Mary's book

4 Practice expressions using the two possessive pronouns *my* and *your*.

Ask: "How old is your mother?"
       "How old is your father?"
       "How old is your sister?"
       (*Continue.*)

Students answer: "My mother is_____ years old."
                   "My father is_____ years old."
                   (*Continue.*)

5 Pick up one of the picture cards for this lesson, ask questions about it, and let other students answer.

6 Walk around the room and ask questions about the people and things. Ask other students to answer.

7 Go to the blackboard and compose a sentence of your own. Let other students or the teacher decide if it is a correct English sentence.

Lesson Eight

Hair, Eyes, Clothes, and Colors

LISTENING DRILL

Step 1. Listen to your teacher pronounce the words below several times.

Step 2. Listen to your teacher say each word and decide if it is number 6, 7, 8, or 9.

Step 3. Answer with the number when the teacher pronounces the words.

6	7	8	9
cod	cawed	code	cooed

READING

We know two families in Centerville now: the Baker family and the Hill family. There are six people in the Baker family: Mr. Baker, Mrs. Baker, Joan, Peter, Tom, and Carol. There are four people in the Hill family: Mr. Hill, Mrs. Hill, Jerry, and Linda. Mrs. Hill's sister, Mrs. Carter, and Mrs. Carter's daughter, Sharon, live with the Hills.

Mr. Baker has brown hair and brown eyes. Mrs. Baker has blond hair and blue eyes. Peter and Joan have blond hair and blue eyes, too. They look like Mrs. Baker. Tom and Carol have brown hair and brown eyes. They look like Mr. Baker.

Mr. and Mrs. Hill both have black hair and brown eyes. Jerry and Linda have black hair and brown eyes, too. Jerry and Linda look like their mother and father.

We are going to talk about the color of hair and eyes in this lesson. We are going to talk about clothes and the color of clothes, too.

"YES OR NO" QUESTIONS

Give the correct short answer.

1. Are there six people in the Baker family?
2. Are there ten people in the Hill family?
3. Does Mr. Baker have brown hair and brown eyes?
4. Does Mrs. Baker have brown hair and brown eyes?
5. Do Peter and Joan have blond hair?
6. Is Peter's father an auto mechanic?
7. Is Jerry's father an auto mechanic?
8. Is Sharon's mother a teacher?

"OR" QUESTIONS

1. Is Mrs. Baker's hair blond or brown?
2. Does Mr. Baker have blue eyes or brown eyes?
3. Is Jerry's father a postman or an auto mechanic?
4. Is Linda a student or a secretary?

"QUESTION WORD" QUESTIONS

1. What color are Peter's eyes?
2. What color is Peter's hair?

3. What color are Carol's eyes?
4. What color is Carol's hair?
5. What color are your eyes?
6. What color is your hair?

CONVERSATIONS

1   A. What color is Tom's hair?
    B. His hair is brown.
    A. What color are his eyes?
    B. His eyes are brown, too.
    A. Carol's eyes are blue, aren't they?
    B. Yes, they are, and her hair is blond.

2   A. What color is Jerry's shirt?
    B. His shirt is blue.
    A. What color are his pants?
    B. His pants are grey.
    A. What color are his shoes?
    B. They're grey, too.

3   A. Who is that girl?
    B. That's Linda Hill.
    A. Please describe her.
    B. She has black hair and brown eyes.
    A. What color are her clothes?
    B. Her dress is green, and her shoes are green, too.
    A. Is she a pretty girl?
    B. Yes, she is. She's very pretty.

GRAMMAR NOTES

1. HAS AND HAVE

In this lesson we practice with *has* and *have*. *Has* and *have* are two forms of the same verb. *Has* is used with the third person singular (*he, she, it*). *Have* is used with the first and second persons and with the third person plural (*I, you, we, they*). Here are the patterns:

SINGULAR		PLURAL	
I	have	we	have
you	have	you	have
he	has		
she	has	they	have
it	has		

When names are used the patterns are the same:

SINGULAR		PLURAL	
Joan	has	Joan and Peter	have
Peter	has		
the school	has	the students	have

2. SIMPLE VERB FORM

Have and *has* are examples of the simple verb form. We use the term *simple* in order to clearly distinguish this verb form from the present continuous verb form which you have already studied.

The present continuous verb form is used to talk about the present time. It is often used with the time-word *now:*

Jerry is swimming now.
Mr. Hill is working now.
Linda is writing now.

The simple verb form is essentially timeless. It indicates an action or condition that is generally permanent or habitual.

It is very important to remember this difference between the present continuous and the simple verb forms. You will study and practice this difference in Lesson Eight and in several later lessons.

3. *PANTS*

The word *pants* is always plural. It is used with other plural forms such as *are, these, they,* etc.

These are good pants.
Peter's pants are new.
What color are your pants?

A synonym for *pants* is *trousers.* Some people prefer to use the word *trousers. Pants,* however, is probably now more common in everyday, colloquial speech.

4. POSSESSIVE ADJECTIVES

In this lesson we practice with the forms *my, your, his, her, our,* and *their.* We will call these words "possessive adjectives" in order to distinguish them from the possessive pronouns that you will study later.

Possesive adjectives are similar in function to the possessive nouns that you studied in Lesson Seven. They indicate that something is owned (possessed) by someone. There is a possessive adjective that corresponds to each of the subject pronouns:

POSSESSIVE ADJECTIVE—SUBJECT PRONOUN		*POSSESSIVE ADJECTIVE—SUBJECT PRONOUN*	
I	my	we	our
you	your	you	your
he	his ⎫		
she	her ⎬	they	their
it	its ⎭		

Notice how these forms are used in sentences:

I have a book.	It is my book.
You have a book.	It is your book.
She has a book.	It is her book.
He has a book.	It is his book.
We have books.	They are our books.
They have books.	They are their books.

5. COLORS

In this lesson we practice with these words for color: *black, white, blue, red, green, yellow, gray,* and *brown.* We also use the word *blond* which is generally used only to refer to hair color.

Words for color can be used as nouns or adjectives. In this lesson you will practice using them only as adjectives. Notice that in English we do not often use the word *color* after a color word.

Common   His shirt is red.
Not common   His shirt is a red color.

6. WHAT COLOR?

To ask about colors we often use the expression *what color:*

What color is his shirt?
What color is her hair?
What color are her eyes?
What color are his pants?

7. HAIR

Hair referring to the hair on our heads is a "non-count" noun. It is used with the linking verb *is* and other singular forms. You will study more about "count" and "non-count" nouns later.

8 HAVE OR HAS WITH AGE

In Spanish and some other languages it is common to use the equivalent of the English verb *have* when talking about age. This is not common usage in English and is incorrect.

CORRECT	INCORRECT
Jerry is seventeen years old.	Jerry has seventeen years.
I am twenty years old.	I have twenty years.
He is forty years old.	He has forty years.
Sharon is five.	Sharon has five years.

Remember to use forms of *be* (am, is, are) when speaking of age.

59

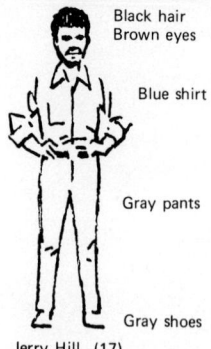

Black hair
Brown eyes

Blue shirt

Gray pants

Gray shoes

Jerry Hill (17)

60

Black hair
Brown eyes

Green dress

Green shoes

Linda Hill (14)

61

Brown hair
Brown eyes

White shirt

White pants

White shoes

Tom Baker (16)

62

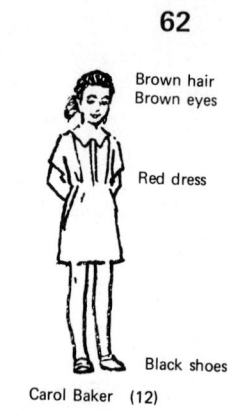

Brown hair
Brown eyes

Red dress

Black shoes

Carol Baker (12)

63

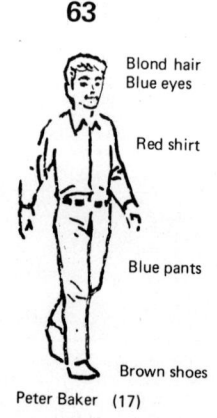

Blond hair
Blue eyes

Red shirt

Blue pants

Brown shoes

Peter Baker (17)

64

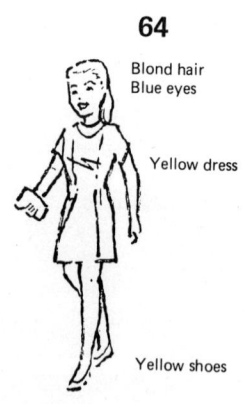

Blond hair
Blue eyes

Yellow dress

Yellow shoes

Joan Baker (20)

PICTURE DRILLS

1 Color the pictures on chart eight according to the colors given.

2 Review the numbers from 1 to 58. Use the pictures from Lessons One through Seven.

3 Practice the numbers 59 to 64.

59. fifty-nine   62. sixty-two
60. sixty   63. sixty-three
61. sixty-one   64. sixty-four

4 Review and practice asking about and telling age:

1. How old is Jerry?   He is seventeen years old.
2. How old is Linda?   She is fourteen years old.
3. How old is Tom?   He is sixteen years old.
4. How old is Carol?   She is twelve years old.
5. How old is Peter?   He is seventeen years old.
6. How old is Joan?   She is twenty years old.

5 Practice statements with the simple verb *has* and words for hair color.

1. Jerry has black hair.   4. Carol has brown hair.
2. Linda has black hair.   5. Peter has blond hair.
3. Tom has brown hair.   6. Joan has blond hair.

6 Practice statements with a plural subject and the simple verb *have.*

1. Jerry and Linda have black hair.
2. Tom and Carol have brown hair.
3. Peter and Joan have blond hair.

7 Practice statements with the simple verb *has* and words for eye color.

1. Jerry has brown eyes.   4. Carol has brown eyes.
2. Linda has brown eyes.   5. Peter has blue eyes.
3. Tom has brown eyes.   6. Joan has blue eyes.

8 Practice statements with a plural subject and *have.*

1. Jerry and Linda have brown eyes.
2. Tom and Carol have brown eyes.
3. Peter and Joan have blue eyes.

9 Review and practice statements with possessive nouns.

1. hair	Jerry's hair is black.
2. eyes	Jerry's eyes are brown.
3. shirt	Jerry's shirt is blue.
4. pants	Jerry's pants are gray.
5. shoes	Jerry's shoes are gray.
6. hair	Linda's hair is black.
7. eyes	Linda's eyes are brown.
8. dress	Linda's dress is green.
9. shoes	Linda's shoes are green.
10. hair	Tom's hair is brown.
11. eyes	Tom's eyes are brown.

(*Continue.*)

10 Practice statements with possessive adjectives.

1. hair	His hair is black.
2. eyes	His eyes are brown.
3. shirt	His shirt is blue.
4. pants	His pants are gray.
5. shoes	His shoes are gray.
6. hair	Her hair is black.
7. eyes	Her eyes are brown.
8. dress	Her dress is green.

(*Continue.*)

11 Practice questions with *what color* and answers with possessive adjectives.

1. What color is Jerry's hair?	His hair is black.
2. What color are Jerry's eyes?	His eyes are brown.
3. What color is Jerry's shirt?	His shirt is blue.
4. What color are Jerry's pants?	His pants are gray.
5. What color are Jerry's shoes?	His shoes are gray.
6. What color is Linda's hair?	Her hair is black.
7. What color are Linda's eyes?	Her eyes are brown.
8. What color is Linda's dress?	Her dress is green.

(*Continue.*)

12 Summary Drill.   Practice a pattern of related statements.

Jerry's hair is black, his eyes are brown, his shirt is blue, his pants are gray, and his shoes are gray.

Linda's hair is black, her eyes are brown, her dress is green, and her shoes are green.

SUBSTITUTION DRILLS

1 Practice using the simple verb forms *have* and *has* in statements.

Examples: I/a book   *I have a book.*
you/a pencil *You have a pencil.*
he/a red shirt *He has a red shirt.*

1. I/ a pencil
2. she/a blue dress
3. they/a big house
4. we/a good class
5. he/a pretty sister
6. you/a beautiful sister
7. Jerry/a small room
8. Linda/black hair
9. Jerry and Linda/brown eyes
10. he/an intelligent brother
11. Mr. Baker/a car
12. they/four children

2 Practice affirmative statements with possessive adjectives.

Examples: my *This is my book.*
your *This is your book.*
his *This is his book.*

1. my
2. your
3. his
4. her
5. our
6. your
7. their

3 Practice questions with possessive adjectives.

Examples: my *Is this my pen?*
your *Is this your pen?*
his *Is this his pen?*

1. my
2. your
3. his
4. her
5. our
6. your
7. their

4 Practice negative statements with possessive adjectives.

Examples: my *That isn't my house.*
your *That isn't your house.*
his *That isn't his house.*

1. my
2. your
3. his
4. her
4. our
6. your
7. their

Note. Drills 2, 3, and 4 can be repeated using other nouns.

5 Practice questions with possessive adjectives and the expression *what color.*

Examples: your shirt *What color is your shirt?*
 your shoes *What color are your shoes?*

1. his shirt	7. your shoes
2. her dress	8. my book
3. my eyes	9. his pants
4. my hair	10. her dress
5. their house	11. our books
6. our school	12. your hair

6 Practice statements with possessive adjectives and words for color.

Examples: his shirt/yellow *His shirt is yellow.*
 her shoes/green *Her shoes are green.*

1. her dress/green	7. their books/blue
2. his shoes/brown	8. your eyes/blue
3. his hat/black	9. her hair/blond
4. my shoes/black	10. my pencil/yellow
5. his pants/gray	11. his pencil/red
6. our house/white	12. your hair/black

7 Practice statements with possessive adjectives and review family words and present continuous verb forms.

Examples: his sister/dance *His sister is dancing now.*
 her father/work *Her father is working now.*

1. his brother/study	9. my sister/write
2. my father/work	10. our father/work
3. his wife/cook	11. their children/study
4. his son/swim	12. their son/sing
5. his daughter/paint	13. my aunt/eat
6. her uncle/teach	14. his students/read
7. my mother/clean	15. her husband/work
8. my father/work	16. her sister/teach

TRANSFORMATION DRILLS

1 Change from *I* (first person) to *he* (third person).

Example: First Person *I have a book.*
 Third Person *He has a book.*

1. I have a pencil.	7. I have two brothers and three sisters.
2. I have brown hair.	8. I have a good old car.
3. I have brown eyes.	9. I have a blue shirt and gray pants.
4. I have two new books.	10. I have a small house in this town.
5. I have three sisters.	11. I have an intelligent teacher.
6. I have a good wife.	12. I have a new blue shirt.

2 Change the italic possessive nouns to possessive adjectives.

Examples:	Possessive noun	*Peter's* shirt is red.
	Possessive adjective	*His shirt is red.*

	Possessive noun	*Linda's* eyes are brown.
	Possessive adjective	*Her eyes are brown.*

1. *Jerry's* pants are gray.
2. *Carol's* hair is brown.
3. *Peter and Joan's* eyes are blue.
4. *Tom's* mother is cooking now.
5. *Tom's* father is working now.
6. *Mr. and Mrs. Baker's* children are in school.
7. Where is *Jerry's* sister?
8. Is *Linda's* brother a handsome boy?
9. *Carol's* dress is red.
10. *The Hills'* house is near the school.
11. *Jerry's* father has a car.
12. *Jerry's* aunt is teaching English.
13. Sharon is *Jerry's* cousin.
14. *Linda's* father is working in the Centerville Post Office.
15. She is *Peter's* friend.
16. *Jerry's* aunt is an intelligent woman.
17. *Mr. Hill's* son is a tall boy.
18. *Mr. Hill's* wife is a good mother.

3 Change these statements to questions.

Example:	Statement	Jerry's sister is studying now.
	Question	*Is Jerry's sister studying now?*

1. My eyes are brown.
2. Peter's hair is blond.
3. Mr. Hill's wife is cleaning in the living room.
4. Peter and Jerry are good friends.
5. The tall man is eating.
6. She is cooking in the kitchen.
7. Tom is playing the guitar now.
8. Mr. Baker is an auto mechanic.
9. Those men are working now.
10. Mr. Baker is a good man.
11. These are cups.
12. These are Mrs. Baker's cups.
13. Those are her plates.
14. These are her pans.
15. The store is near the bank.
16. The Bakers' house is in Centerville.
17. Centerville is a large town in the United States.
18. English is a difficult language.

4 Change from affirmative to negative. Use the contracted form with the verb.

Example:	Affirmative	He is a young man.
	Negative	*He isn't a young man.*

1. She is working now.
2. Peter is typing a letter now.
3. Linda is Jerry's mother.
4. Jerry's shoes are red.
5. My hair is green.
6. Your eyes are red.
7. Mr. and Mrs. Hill's children are working now.
8. Mrs. Carter is Mrs. Baker's sister.
9. We are studying Spanish now.
10. My mother's brother is a postman.
11. English is very easy.
12. I am a bad student.
13. This school is in Centerville.
14. Mrs. Baker's husband is dead.
15. Sharon is Mrs. Hill's daughter.
16. Mrs. Baker's dishes are in the living room.
17. Peter is forty-one years old.
18. Peter's hair and eyes are green.

WRITING PRACTICE

Choose one word for each space in the paragraph.

　　　We know two families in (1)＿＿＿＿＿＿＿＿ now; the Baker family and the Hill (2)＿＿＿＿＿＿＿＿ . There are six people in the Baker family; Mr. Baker, Mrs. Baker, Joan, Peter, Tom, and Carol. There are four (3) ＿＿＿＿＿＿＿＿ in the Hill family; Mr. Hill, Mrs. Hill, Jerry, and Linda. Mr. Baker (4) ＿＿＿＿＿＿＿＿ brown hair and brown eyes. Mrs. Baker has blond hair and blue (5)＿＿＿＿＿＿＿＿ . Peter and Joan have blond hair and blue eyes, too. They look like Mrs. Baker. Tom and Carol (6)＿＿＿＿＿＿＿＿ brown hair and brown eyes. They look like Mr. Baker. Mr. (7)＿＿＿＿＿＿＿＿ Mrs. Hill both have black hair and brown eyes. Jerry and Linda have black hair and brown eyes, (8)＿＿＿＿＿＿＿＿ . They look like their mother and father.

SITUATIONAL PRACTICE

1 Ask several students to go to the front of the room and describe their hair and eyes to the class. Ask them to use the possessive adjective *my.*

　　　　　　　Examples:　　"My hair is black."
　　　　　　　　　　　　　"My eyes are brown."
　　　　　　　　　　　　　(*Continue.*)

2 Describe other student's hair and eyes to the class. Use possessive nouns.

　　　　　　　Examples:　　"Robert's hair is black."
　　　　　　　　　　　　　"Mary's hair is brown."
　　　　　　　　　　　　　"John's eyes are blue."
　　　　　　　　　　　　　"Martha's hair is blond."
　　　　　　　　　　　　　(*Continue.*)

3 Describe other student's hair and eyes. Use possessive adjectives.

　　　　　　　Examples:　　"His hair is brown."
　　　　　　　　　　　　　"His eyes are black."
　　　　　　　　　　　　　"Her hair is blond."
　　　　　　　　　　　　　"Her eyes are brown."
　　　　　　　　　　　　　(*Continue.*)

4 Tell the class about your clothes using the possessive adjective *my.*

(*You may need to learn a few more words for clothes and colors to do this game.*)

5 Play a guessing game. Describe a student in the class. Talk about his hair, eyes, and clothes. Let other students try to guess which student you are describing.

6 Review lessons one through eight by using all the pictures. Ask different questions about the people and things in the pictures.

"Who is he?"   "He is Mr. Smith."
"What is he doing?"   "He is eating."
"Is he a man or a boy?"   "He is a man."
"Where is he eating?"   "He is eating in a restaurant."
"What is this?"   "It is a table."
"What are these?"   "They are dishes."
(*Continue.*)

Lesson Nine

The Supermarket

LISTENING DRILL

Step 1. Listen to your teacher pronounce the words below several times.
Step 2. Listen to your teacher say each word and decide if it is number 7, 8, 9, or 10.
Step 3. Answer with the number when the teacher pronounces the words.

7	8	9	10
cawed	code	cooed	could

READING

Mrs. Baker usually goes to the supermarket every Saturday morning. She buys the food that she needs for the week. Mr. Baker usually goes, too. He drives the car and carries the heavy things.

Before she goes to the supermarket, Mrs. Baker looks in the refrigerator and cabinets. She sees what she has and what she needs. She writes the things she needs on a piece of paper. At the supermarket she buys the things on the piece of paper. She usually buys some other things, too.

There are many different kinds of food: meat, bread, milk, coffee, eggs, tomatoes, butter, and so on. You are going to practice with some of the words for food in this lesson.

"YES OR NO" QUESTIONS
Give the correct short answer.

1. Does Mrs. Baker usually go to the supermarket every Saturday morning?
2. Does Mr. Baker usually go with her?
3. Does Mrs. Baker drive the car?
4. Does Mr. Baker drive the car?
5. Are there many different kinds of food?
6. Is meat a food?
7. Are tomatoes a kind of food?
8. Are shoes a kind of food?

"OR" QUESTIONS

1. Does Mrs. Baker go to the supermarket every Saturday or every Sunday?
2. Does Mr. Baker usually drive the car or does Mrs. Baker usually drive it?
3. Does Mrs. Baker buy food at the supermarket or does she buy clothes?

"QUESTION WORD" QUESTIONS

1. Where does Mrs. Baker usually go every Saturday?
2. Who usually goes with her?
3. Who usually drives the car?
4. What does Mrs. Baker buy at the supermarket?

CONVERSATIONS

1   *(Mrs. Baker is talking to Mr. Baker.)*

A. Today is Saturday.
B. Yes, I know. Are you going to the supermarket?
A. Yes, I am. Do you want to come?
B. Yes. What do you need?
A. Oh, meat, bread, eggs, and some other things.
B. All right. We need some coffee, too.
A. I am writing everything we need on a piece of paper.

2   *(Two people in the supermarket see Mr. and Mrs. Baker.)*

A. Who is that woman?
B. That's Mrs. Baker. She is Peter's mother.
A. Oh yes, that man is her husband, isn't he?
B. Yes, that's Mr. Baker.
A. They usually come to the supermarket every Saturday, don't they?
B. Yes, they do. I see them here every Saturday.

3   *(Tom is talking to his sister, Carol.)*

A. Do you have your books?
B. Yes, I do. Here they are.
A. Do you have your pencil and paper?
B. I have a pencil, but I don't have any paper.
A. I have a lot of paper. Take some.
B. Thanks a lot.

GRAMMAR NOTES

1. SIMPLE VERB FORM (Continued)

In Lesson Eight we practiced with the simple verb *have* (and *has*). The simple verb form is essentially timeless. It is used to describe an action or state that is permanent or habitual. Remember that the simple verb does not usually indicate present time. To indicate present time, English generally uses the present continuous verb form.

The simple verb changes form for the third person singular. Most verbs add *s* for the third person singular. This *s* does *not* mean plural. Notice these examples:

GO	*NEED*	*DRIVE*
I go	I need	I drive
you go	you need	you drive
he goes	he needs	he drives
she goes	she needs	she drives
we go	we need	we drive
you go	you need	you drive
they go	they need	they drive

2. QUESTIONS WITH THE SIMPLE VERB FORM

To make questions with the simple verb form we add a special auxiliary verb. This auxiliary is *do*. For the third person singular, the *s* is removed from the verb and the auxiliary changes to *does*.

Do I go?	Do I need?	Do I drive?
Do you go?	Do you need?	Do you drive?
Does he go?	Does he need?	Does he drive?
Does she go?	Does she need?	Does she drive?
Do we go?	Do we need?	Do we drive?
Do you go?	Do you need?	Do you drive?
Do they go?	Do they need?	Do they drive?

3. NEGATIVE FORMS OF THE SIMPLE VERB

Negative forms are made with the auxiliary *do* or *does* and *not.*

I do not go	I do not need	I do not drive
You do not go	You do not need	You do not drive
He does not go	He does not need	He does not drive
She does not go	She does not need	She does not drive
We do not go	We do not need	We do not drive
You do not go	You do not need	You do not drive
They do not go	They do not need	They do not drive

4. CONTRACTIONS

The contractions *don't* and *doesn't* are frequently used in conversation.

I don't need any coffee.
He doesn't have a pencil.
We don't want that book.

5. COUNT AND NON-COUNT NOUNS

Some things we can count. Some things we cannot count. Nouns for things that we can count are called *count nouns*. Nouns for things that we cannot count are called *non-count nouns.*

Count nouns have singular and plural forms. Non-count nouns have only one form. They are neither singular nor plural. Non-count nouns are used with *is* and other "singular" forms.

COUNT NOUNS		NON-COUNT NOUNS
egg	eggs	bread
potato	potatoes	flour
banana	bananas	coffee
tomato	tomatoes	meat
book	books	butter
pencil	pencils	rice
house	houses	milk
man	men	cheese

6. SOME AND ANY

Some and *any* usually come before plural or non-count nouns. They often replace *a* which comes before singular nouns only. Notice these examples:

SINGULAR	PLURAL
I need a book.	I need some books.
He has a potato.	He has some potatoes.
She wants a new dress.	She wants some new dresses.

Some is used in affirmative statements. *Any* is used in negative statements:

AFFIRMATIVE	NEGATIVE
I have some milk.	I don't have any milk.
He needs some rice.	He doesn't need any rice.
We have some paper.	We don't have any paper.
Peter has some red shoes.	Peter doesn't have any red shoes.

Either *some* or *any* can be used in affirmative or negative questions:

QUESTIONS

Do you want some bananas?
(or)   Do you want any bananas?

Does he have some blue pants?
(or)   Does he have any blue pants?

Don't you need some coffee?
(or)   Don't you need any coffee?

7. EVERY

When we do something repeatedly at a regular time, it is common to use the word *every* before the time expression. Since this indicates a repeated, habitual action, it is appropriate to use the simple form of the verb in the sentence. Some examples follow:

I go to school every weekday.
We need food every day.
She cooks every night.
They play every afternoon.
Jerry sings every Sunday in church.
They go to the park every weekend.
The bell rings every hour.

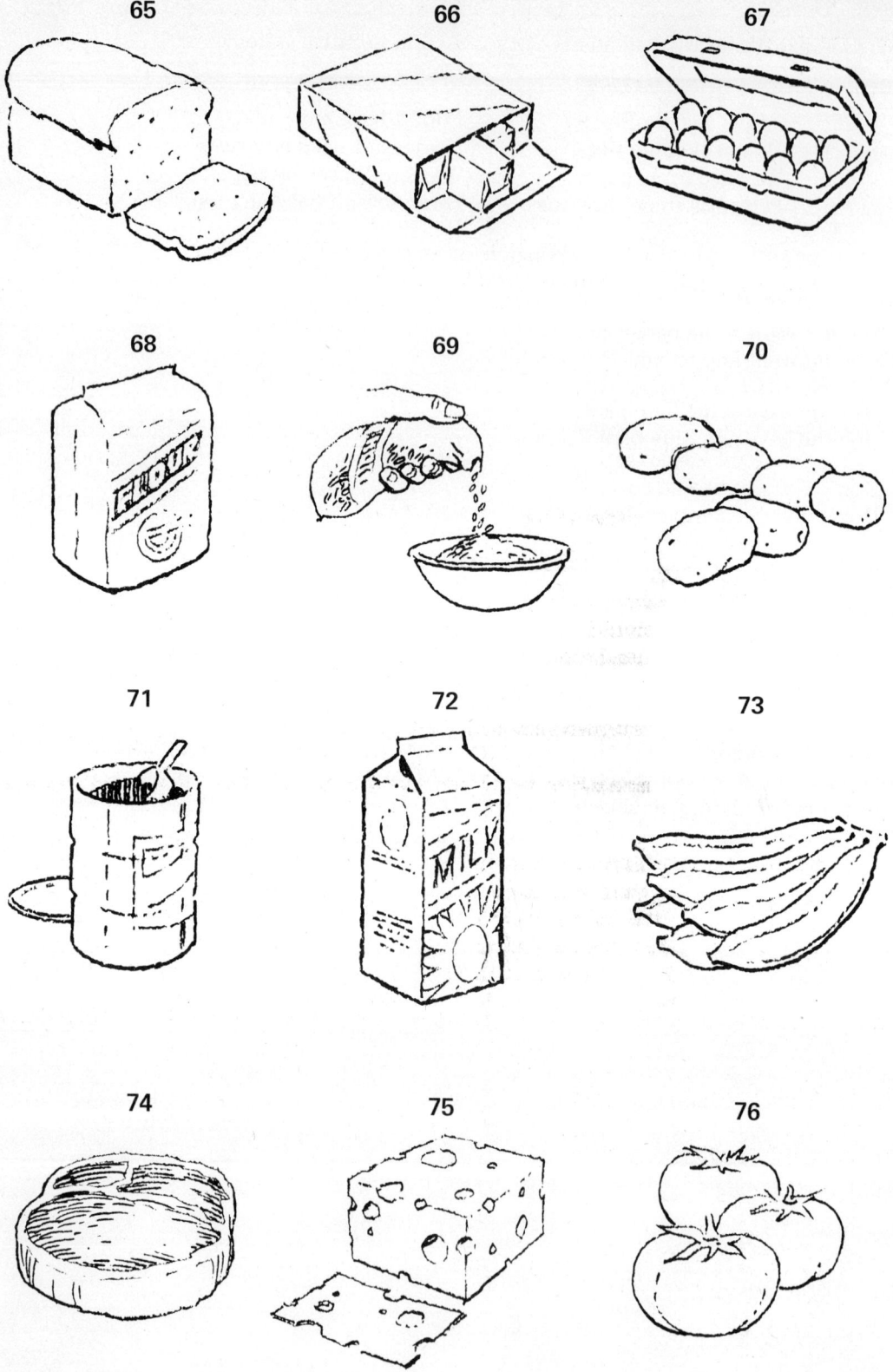

65

66

67

68

69

70

71

72

73

74

75

76

PICTURE DRILLS

1 Review the numbers from 1 to 64.

2 Practice the numbers from 65 to 76.

65. sixty-five	71. seventy-one
66. sixty-six	72. seventy-two
67. sixty-seven	73. seventy-three
68. sixty-eight	74. seventy-four
69. sixty-nine	75. seventy-five
70. seventy	76. seventy-six

3 Practice the names of the foods in the pictures.

1. bread	7. milk
2. flour	8. cheese
3. coffee	9. eggs
4. meat	10. potatoes
5. butter	11. bananas
6. rice	12. tomatoes

4 Practice statements with the names of the foods and review adjectives for color.

(You may color the pictures in the book with crayons or marking pens.)

1. This bread is white.	7. This coffee is brown.
2. This butter is yellow.	8. This milk is white.
3. These eggs are white.	9. These bananas are yellow.
4. This flour is white.	10. This meat is red.
5. This rice is white.	11. This cheese is yellow.
6. These potatoes are brown.	12. These tomatoes are red.

5 Practice negative statements with the simple verb *have*, the word *any*, and the names of foods.

1. Mrs. Baker doesn't have any bread.
2. Mrs. Baker doesn't have any butter.
3. Mrs. Baker doesn't have any eggs.
4. Mrs. Baker doesn't have any flour.
   (Continue.)

6 Practice affirmative statements with the simple verb *need* and *some*. (*need* becomes *needs* for the third person singular.)

1. Mrs. Baker needs some bread.
2. Mrs. Baker needs some butter.
3. Mrs. Baker needs some eggs.
4. Mrs. Baker needs some flour.
   (Continue.)

7 Practice a pattern of related negative and affirmative statements.

1. Mrs. Baker doesn't have any bread. She needs some bread.
2. Mrs. Baker doesn't have any butter. She needs some butter.
3. Mrs. Baker doesn't have any eggs. She needs some eggs.
4. Mrs. Baker doesn't have any flour. She needs some flour.
   (*Continue.*)

8 Practice questions with *have* and negative short answers.

1. Does Mrs. Baker have some bread?   No, she doesn't.
2. Does Mrs. Baker have some butter?   No, she doesn't.
3. Does Mrs. Baker have some eggs?   No, she doesn't.
4. Does Mrs. Baker have some flour?   No, she doesn't.
   (*Continue.*)

9 Practice questions with *need* and affirmative answers.

1. Does Mrs. Baker need some bread?   Yes, she does.
2. Does Mrs. Baker need some butter?   Yes, she does.
3. Does Mrs. Baker need some eggs?   Yes, she does.
4. Does Mrs. Baker need some flour?   Yes, she does.
   (*Continue.*)

10 Practice questions with *have* or *need* and affirmative or negative short answers.

1. Does Mrs. Baker have some bread?   No, she doesn't.
2. Does Mrs. Baker need some bread?   Yes, she does.
3. Does Mrs. Baker have some butter?   No, she doesn't.
4. Does Mrs. Baker need some butter?   Yes, she does.
   (*Continue.*)

Note. Drills 5 through 10 can be varied and repeated several times by changing the subject. Ask students to pretend to be Mrs. Baker and do the drills using the pronouns *I* and *you* and their related forms. Then do the drills using *Mr. and Mrs. Baker* for the subject and the pronoun *they* with its related forms.

11 The teacher will show the picture and say the word. The students respond by saying *count* or *non-count*.

TEACHER	STUDENTS
bread	non-count
butter	non-count
eggs	count
flour	non-count

(*Continue.*)

Repeat this drill saying the words without showing the pictures.

SUBSTITUTION DRILLS

1 Practice affirmative statements with the simple verb form and *some*. Use the verb *need*.

Examples: I/milk   *I need some milk.*
he/milk   *He needs some milk.*
you/eggs *You need some eggs.*
she/eggs *She needs some eggs.*

1. I/eggs
2. he/pencils
3. she/butter
4. they/tomatoes
5. we/coffee
6. I/rice
7. we/meat
8. she/bananas
9. Mrs. Baker/potatoes
10. Mr. Baker/coffee
11. Carol/butter
12. Joan/bread
13. Mrs. Hill/flour
14. Jerry and Peter/milk

2 Practice negative statements with the simple verb *want* and the word *any*.

Examples: I/coffee   *I don't want any coffee.*
he/coffee   *He doesn't want any coffee.*
they/paper *They don't want any paper.*

1. she/eggs
2. we/bananas
3. they/meat
4. I/tomatoes
5. Linda/bread
6. she/milk
7. Jerry/potatoes
8. Jerry and Peter/rice
9. they/rice
10. Linda/milk
11. Carol/coffee
12. Sharon/milk
13. Linda and Carol/cheese
14. Mr. and Mrs. Baker/tomatoes

3 Practice questions with the simple verb *have* and *some* or *any*. Notice that the questions with *some* have almost the same meaning as the questions with *any*. *Some* or *any* may be used in questions.

Examples: you/some milk   *Do you want some milk?*
you/any milk   *Do you want any milk?*

he/some coffee *Does he want some coffee?*
he/any coffee   *Does he want any coffee?*

1. he/some meat
2. he/any meat
3. she/some rice
4. she/any rice
5. you/some books
6. you/any books
7. they/some shoes
8. they/any shoes
9. he/some old shoes
10. he/any old shoes
11. we/some paper
12. we/any paper
13. we/any white paper
14. you/some red pencils

4 Complete the sentences using *some* or *any*.

Examples: He has _____*some*_____ books.
She doesn't have _____*any*_____ books.

1. I have_____ books.
2. You don't have_____ paper.
3. We need_____ food.
4. Mrs. Baker needs_____ meat.
5. She doesn't need_____ bread.
6. I don't have_____ pencils.

7. Tom doesn't have_____ paper.
8. He wants_____ coffee.
9. I need_____ new shoes.
10. He has_____ new blue pants.
11. Mr. Baker wants_____ good black shoes.
12. He doesn't have_____ red shirts.

5 Complete the sentences using *don't* or *doesn't*.

Examples: He _____*doesn't*_____ have any books.
I _____*don't*_____ have any books.
You _____*don't*_____ need any coffee.
Mrs. Baker _____*doesn't*_____ have any meat.

1. She_____ have any coffee.
2. I_____ need any milk.
3. We_____ want any cheese.
4. She_____ go to the store on Sunday.
5. The children_____ go to school on Saturday and Sunday.
6. Linda_____ have a car.
7. Peter_____ need any new black shoes.
8. I_____ have any paper.

9. Tom and Peter_____ need any new clothes.
10. We_____ study Spanish in this class.
11. The Bakers_____ live in New York.
12. Mr. Baker_____ work in the Centerville Post Office.
13. I_____ understand English very well.
14. You_____ know that man.

6 Practice the simple verb *go* (*goes*) with the words for the days of the week:

Examples: she/Saturday
She goes to the store every Saturday.

I/Monday
I go to the store every Monday.

1. he/Saturday
2. I/Monday
3. you/Wednesday
4. he/Wednesday
5. she/Thursday
6. we/Friday
7. they/Saturday
8. Mrs. Baker/Saturday
9. Mrs. Hill/Tuesday
10. Jerry/Monday
11. Peter/Tuesday
12. Linda/Wednesday
13. Tom/Thursday
14. Carol/Friday

TRANSFORMATION DRILLS

1 Change from first person (*I*) to third person (*he*).

Examples: First person   I need some bread.
          Third person   *He needs some bread.*

          First person   I want some coffee.
          Third person   *He wants some coffee.*

1. I need some coffee.
2. I want some tomatoes.
3. I have some books.
4. I drive the car.
5. I go to school every day.
6. I have some books.
7. I want some butter.
8. I carry the heavy things.
9. I need a new shirt.
10. I want some new black shoes.
11. I have one brother and two sisters.
12. I study English in school every day.
13. I swim in the pool every Saturday.
14. I sing in church every Sunday.

2 Change from affirmative to negative.

Examples: Affirmative   Mrs. Baker wants some coffee.
          Negative   *Mrs. Baker doesn't want any coffee.*

          Affirmative   I need some new shoes.
          Negative   *I don't need any new shoes.*

1. Mr. Baker wants some coffee.
2. Peter wants some paper.
3. Joan needs some new shoes.
4. I have a new dress.
5. Linda has a new hat.
6. Peter's sister has some new shoes.
7. Jerry's father has a new car.
8. Jerry's father has some new pants.
9. Linda's cousin wants some milk.
10. My sister works in an office.
11. Her mother has a big kitchen.
12. Their children want some dinner.
13. Joan is a housewife.
14. I am a postman.
15. Mr. Smith is a poor man.
16. English is a very easy language.
17. We study Spanish in this class.
18. We are studying Spanish now.
19. Tom Baker speaks Spanish.
20. The Baker children speak Spanish.

3 Change the *italicized* noun from *singular* to *plural*. Change *a* to *some* or *any*.

Examples: Singular   He has *a book*.
          Plural   He has *some books*.

          Singular   I don't have *a pen*.
          Plural   I don't have *any pens*.

1. He has *a desk*.
2. I don't have *a pencil*.
3. Jerry doesn't have *a brother*.
4. My sister doesn't have *a book*.
5. Peter's father has *a* new *book*.
6. Linda needs *a cup*.
7. Mrs. Baker's sister wants *a* new *dress*.
8. I need *a cup*.
9. They don't have *a knife*.
10. Carol's cousin needs *an egg*.
11. We write *a sentence* every day.
12. His friend has *a picture*.

4 Change these statements to questions.

Examples:	Statement	You have some books.
	Question	*Do you have some books?*
	Statement	He has some books.
	Question	*Does he have some books?*

1. You have some pencils.
2. They have some pencils.
3. He has some pencils.
4. She has some pencils.
5. They have some pencils.
6. Peter has some blue pants.
7. Mrs. Baker needs some rice.
8. You want some coffee.
9. He wants some coffee.
10. She goes to the supermarket every Saturday.
11. They go to the supermarket every Saturday.
12. Mr. Hill works in the Centerville Post Office.
13. Sharon's mother teaches in the Centerville High School.
14. Peter studies Spanish in high school.
15. We go to school every weekday.
16. English is difficult.
17. We are speaking English now.
18. We speak English every day.
19. Peter speaks English.
20. Peter speaks a little Spanish, too.

WRITING PRACTICE

Choose one word for each blank space.

Mrs. Baker usually (1)_____ to the supermarket every Saturday morning. She buys the food that she needs for the week. Mr. (2)_____ usually goes, too. He drives the (3)_____ and carries the heavy things.

Before she goes to the (4)_____ , Mrs. Baker looks in the refrigerator (5)_____ cabinets. She sees what she has and what she (6)_____ . She writes down the things that she needs on a piece of (7)_____ . At the supermarket, she buys the things on the piece of paper. She usually (8)_____ some other things, too.

SITUATIONAL PRACTICE

1 Review Lessons One to Nine by asking questions about all the picture cards.

2 Ask students questions with *have.*

For example, "Do you have a (pencil)?" The students give short answers; "Yes, I do." or "No, I don't." Avoid asking questions that might embarrass some students. (Notice that the answer; "Yes, I do." or "No, I don't." is more common than "Yes, I have." or "No, I haven't." in American English.)

3 When students answer "No, I don't." to questions in 9.2, you can ask another question: "Do you want a *(pencil)*?" Again they answer "Yes, I do." or "No, I don't."

4 Ask several students to come to the front of the room. Ask questions about their clothes using the simple verb *have*.

"Does Mary have a blue dress?"
"Does John have brown pants?"
"Do John and Mary have black shoes?"
(*Continue.*)

Let other students give short answers such as:

"Yes, she does."	"No, he doesn't."
"Yes, he does."	"Yes, they do."
"No, she doesn't."	"No, they don't."
(*Continue.*)	

5 Play a guessing game using the verb *have* (*has*).

Describe a student using expressions such as:

"He has black hair. He has brown eyes. He has a blue shirt today. He has blue pants. He has black shoes." (*Continue.*)

Then ask "Who is he?" and let students guess the name.

Lesson Ten

LISTENING DRILL

Step 1. Listen to your teacher pronounce the words below several times.
Step 2. Listen to your teacher say each word and decide if it is number 1, 2, 3, or 4.
Step 3. Answer with the number when the teacher pronounces the words.

1	2	3	4
code	cooed	could	cud

READING

You remember Peter Baker, of course. Peter lives in the town of Centerville in the United States. He lives with his father, mother, brother, and two sisters.

Peter is a student in the Centerville High School. He goes to school every weekday—Monday, Tuesday, Wednesday, Thursday, and Friday. He doesn't go to school on Saturday or Sunday.

Every weekday Peter does about the same things. He gets up, dresses, eats breakfast, and goes to school every morning. He attends classes in school every day. Every afternoon he goes home and listens to music. Every evening he eats dinner with his family and watches television for an hour or two. Then he does his homework and after that he takes a bath. Then he goes to bed.

Peter usually gets up at seven o'clock. He usually goes to bed about ten or ten-thirty. What time do you usually get up? What time do you usually go to bed?

In this lesson we are going to talk about the things that people do every day. We are going to talk about time, too.

"YES OR NO" QUESTIONS

Give the correct short answer.

1. Does Peter live in Centerville?
2. Is Peter a student?
3. Does Peter go to school every weekday?
4. Does he go to school on Saturday and Sunday?
5. Does Peter eat breakfast every morning?
6. Does he attend classes at school?
7. Does he cook dinner every afternoon?
8. Does he take a bath every night?

"OR" QUESTIONS

1. Is Peter a boy or a man?
2. Is he a student or a teacher?
3. Does he work or go to school every day?
4. Does he have one sister or two sisters?

"QUESTION WORD" QUESTIONS

    1. Who does Peter live with?
    2. Where does he live?
    3. What time does he usually get up?
    4. What time does he usually go to bed?

CONVERSATIONS

1   A. What time does Peter usually get up?
    B. He usually gets up at seven o'clock.
    A. What time does he go to bed?
    B. He usually goes to bed about ten or ten-thirty.
    A. Does he go to school every day?
    B. Well. . . .he goes to school every weekday. He doesn't go on Saturday or Sunday.

2   A. What time does Peter eat breakfast?
    B. He usually eats breakfast at seven forty-five.
    A. What time does he eat lunch?
    B. He eats lunch at twelve o'clock.
    A. Does he eat lunch at home?
    B. No, he doesn't. He eats lunch at school.
    A. Where does he eat dinner?
    B. He eats dinner at home with his family.

3   A. Do you study English every day?
    B. Yes, I study it every weekday.
    A. Is English difficult for you?
    B. Sometimes it's difficult. Sometimes it's easy.
    A. Are you studying English now?
    B. No, I'm not. I'm talking to you.
    A. Well, we're speaking English, aren't we?
    B. Yes, that's true. We are speaking and practicing English now.

GRAMMAR NOTES

1. SIMPLE VERB FORM (Continued)

Notice that in this lesson we continue to practice with the simple verb form. The simple verb form is generally used to talk about things that we do frequently or habitually. The sentence "Peter goes to school." indicates that Peter does this frequently or habitually. In this case he does it every weekday. You must not confuse the simple verb form which is used to indicate habitual action with the present continuous verb form which is used to indicate present time action.

SIMPLE VERB FORM	PRESENT CONTINUOUS VERB FORM
(habitual action)	*(present time action)*
He goes to school every day.	He is going to school now.
Peter eats breakfast every day.	Peter is eating breakfast now.
Mr. Baker works every day.	Mr. Baker is working now.
Mrs. Baker cooks every afternoon.	Mrs. Baker is cooking now.
I study English every day.	I am studying English now.
My brother sings in church.	My brother is singing in church.

2. CLOCK TIME

There are 24 hours in a day. There are 60 minutes in an hour. There are 60 seconds in a minute.

English (like most languages) has more than one way to talk about clock time. In this lesson we practice with one of the ways that people talk about time in English. It is a very simple system. In this system we tell the hour and then the minutes:

7:00	seven o'clock
7:10	seven-ten
7:15	seven-fifteen
7:20	seven-twenty
7:30	seven-thirty
7:45	seven-forty-five
8:00	eight o'clock

Your teacher will practice telling time with you. After you have learned this easy system, your teacher may teach you other ways of talking about time. Be sure to pronounce the "o" in "o'clock" with an unstressed (weak) vowel.

3. *HOME*

In this lesson we practice the sentences:

> Peter goes to school.
> (and) Peter goes home.

We do not use the preposition *to* before the word *home*. We say that *home* is here an adverbial and does not take *to*. There are a few other words that do not take *to* in this situation: *downtown*, *here*, and *there* are also adverbials and do not take *to*.

4. *DO* AND *DOES*

In Lesson Nine you learned that *do* and *does* (*does* in the third person singular) are auxiliary verbs used to make questions and negative statements with the simple verb form:

> Does he get up at seven o'clock?   I don't need any tomatoes.
> Do you want some coffee?   He doesn't have any pencils.

Do or *does* can also be used as the main verb in a sentence. They are used this way as a word for action in general and with only a few specific objects of verb action:

> I do that every day.   Mrs. Baker is doing the dishes. (washing the dishes)
> Who does this?   Mrs. Baker does the dishes every night.
> Peter does his homework every night.   Carol helps her mother do the dishes.

We may have sentences with *do* as the main verb, and *do* or *does* as the auxiliary verb:

> Does he do his homework every night?   I don't do that kind of work.
> Do you do that?   She doesn't always do her homework.

This may seem confusing at first. As you practice these kinds of sentences, you will find that they become clear to you.

5. TAG QUESTIONS

In the conversations you have practiced sentences like these:

She is Jerry's mother, isn't she?
The books are new, aren't they?
He gets up at seven o'clock, doesn't he?

These sentences are statements with a question at the end. We call this kind of question a *tag question*. Tag questions are made with an auxiliary verb and a subject pronoun. *When the statement is affirmative, the tag question is negative. When the statement is negative, the tag question is affirmative.*

She is a student, isn't she?
He is a boy, isn't he?
Peter and Jerry are friends, aren't they?
He needs some coffee, doesn't he?
They have a car, don't they?
It is good, isn't it?

She isn't a student, is she?
This isn't easy, is it?
Peter and Jerry aren't friends, are they?
You don't understand, do you?
She isn't studying now, is she?
Peter doesn't get up at six o'clock, does he?

6. TAG QUESTIONS WITH SIMPLE VERB FORMS

Notice that tag questions with simple verb forms use the auxiliary verb *do* or *does*:

He works, doesn't he?
They study, don't they?
She plays the piano, doesn't she?
You understand, don't you?

The negative forms also use *do* or *does*:

She doesn't study, does she?
They don't understand, do they?
You don't work, do you?

77

7:00 (Morning)

78

7:45 (Morning)

79

8:30 (Morning)

80

4:00 (Afternoon)

81

5:00 to 6:00 (Afternoon)

82

6:30 (Evening)

83

7:30 to 8:30 (Evening)

84

8:30 to 10:00 (Evening)

85

10:00 (Night)

86

10:30 (Night)

PICTURE DRILLS

1 Review the numbers from 1 to 76.

2 Practice the numbers from 77 to 86.

77. seventy-seven	82. eighty-two
78. seventy-eight	83. eighty-three
79. seventy-nine	84. eighty-four
80. eighty	85. eighty-five
81. eighty-one	86. eighty-six

3 Practice the simple verb forms for the pictures in Lesson Ten.

1. Peter gets up.	6. He eats dinner.
2. He eats breakfast.	7. He watches television.
3. He goes to school.	8. He does his homework.
4. He goes home.	9. He takes a bath.
5. He listens to music.	10. He goes to bed.

4 Practice the verb forms with time words indicating habitual action.

1. Peter gets up every morning.	6. He eats dinner every evening.
2. He eats breakfast every morning.	7. He watches television every evening.
3. He goes to school every morning.	8. He does his homework every evening.
4. He goes home every afternoon.	9. He takes a bath every night.
5. He listens to music every afternoon.	10. He goes to bed every night.

5 Practice words for clock time.

1. at seven o'clock	6. at seven forty-five
2. at eight-thirty	7. at four o'clock
3. from five to six	8. at six-thirty
4. from seven-thirty to eight-thirty	9. from eight-thirty to ten
5. at ten o'clock	10. at ten-thirty

Note.   You may use a large clock or clock-face to practice additional time words. If a clock face is not available write additional times on the blackboard.

6 Practice the verbs with words for clock time.

1. Peter gets up at seven o'clock.
2. He eats breakfast at seven forty-five.
3. He goes to school at eight-thirty.
4. He goes home at four o'clock.
   (*Continue.*)

7 Practice the verbs with words for clock time and words indicating habitual action.

1. Peter gets up at seven o'clock every morning.
2. He eats breakfast at seven forty-five every morning.
3. He goes to school at eight-thirty every morning.
4. He goes home at four o'clock every afternoon.
   (*Continue.*)

8 Practice questions with the expression *what time* and long answers.

1. What time does Peter get up every morning?
       He gets up at seven o'clock.
2. What time does Peter eat breakfast every morning?
       He eats breakfast at seven forty-five.
3. What time does Peter go to school every morning?
       He goes to school at eight-thirty.
   (*Continue.*)

9 Practice "yes or no" questions and short answers.

1. Does Peter get up at seven o'clock every morning?
       Yes, he does.
2. Does Peter get up at six o'clock every morning?
       No, he doesn't.
3. Does Peter go to school at eight-thirty every morning?
       Yes, he does.
   (*Continue.*)

10 Practice statements with tag questions. Give short answers.

1. Peter gets up at seven o'clock, doesn't he?
       Yes, he does.
2. Peter gets up at six o'clock, doesn't he?
       No, he doesn't.
3. Peter eats breakfast at seven forty-five, doesn't he?
       Yes, he does.
4. Peter eats breakfast at eight o'clock, doesn't he?
       No, he doesn't.
   (*Continue.*)

Note.   Drills 3, 4, and 6 through 10 should be repeated using other subject pronouns (I, you, she, we, and they) or nouns (Tom, Carol, Peter and Tom, etc.).

11 You may use crayons or other colors to color the pictures. Review questions and answers about color.

12 Summary Drill.   Use the pictures for Lessons One to Ten to review the various patterns that have been practiced in Lessons One to Ten.

1. What is this?	It's a bed.
2. Who is he?	He is Peter Baker.
3. What is he doing now?	He is getting up now.
4. Does he get up at seven o'clock every morning?	Yes, he does.
5. Where does he live?	He lives in Centerville.
6. What color are his pants?	His pants are blue.
7. The books are new, aren't they?	Yes, they are.

SUBSTITUTION DRILLS

1 Review and practice statements with the simple verb form.

Examples: he/work/every day   *He works every day.*
I/study/every night   *I study every night.*

1. he/eat/dinner/at 6:30/every evening
2. I/go/to school/at 9:00/every morning
3. she/work/in an office
4. Joan/type/in an office
5. Mr. Baker/work/every day
6. Mr. Hill/get up/at 6:45
7. they/do/their homework/every night
8. he/do/his homework/every night
9. Peter/go/to school/at 8:30
10. we/practice/English/every day

2 Practice questions with the simple verb form.

Examples: he/work/every day   *Does he work every day?*
I/work/every day   *Do I work every day?*

1. you/go/to school/every day
2. he/swim/every afternoon
3. Tom/play/the guitar/every day
4. they/sing/in church/every Sunday
5. Jerry and Peter/study/Spanish/every morning
6. you/go/to bed/at 10:00 every night
7. she/cook/dinner/every night
8. you/do/your homework/every night
9. Carol/paint/beautiful pictures
10. they/need/some coffee

3 Practice negative statements with the simple verb form.

Examples: she/need/any milk   *She doesn't need any milk.*
I/have/any coffee   *I don't have any coffee.*
you/go/to school   *You don't go to school.*

1. I/have/any bread
2. they/get up/at 5:30
3. Peter/work/in an office
4. She/have/a red dress
5. his father/work/in an office
6. her brother/go/to high school
7. my mother/live/in Centerville
8. we/drive/to school in a car
9. Mr. Baker/have three cars
10. Mrs. Carter/watch/television in the afternoon
11. my book/have/many pictures in it
12. this class/have/a television set
13. Jerry's mother/work/in an office
14. Peter and Jerry/go/to school on Saturday and Sunday
15. we/sleep/in this class every day

4 Practice statements with tag questions.

Examples:	he/have/a book	*He has a book, doesn't he?*
	you/need/some rice	*You need some rice, don't you?*
	she/study/English	*She studies English, doesn't she?*

1. she/need/some coffee
2. you/speak/English
3. they/go/to bed at 10:30
4. Mr. Hill/work/in the Centerville Post Office
5. Jerry/have/some black shoes
6. Peter's brother/play/the guitar
7. the Bakers/have/a big house
8. he/need/some paper
9. we/study/English/every day
10. her father/have/some black shoes
11. Sharon's mother/teach/in the Centerville High School
12. Peter's mother/clean/the house/every day

5 Review the present continuous verb form.

Examples:	he/study/now	*He is studying now.*
	I/listen/now	*I am listening now.*

1. they/work/now
2. you/study/English/now
3. she/cook/dinner/now
4. I/practice English/now
5. Peter/swim/now
6. Joan/type/a letter/now
7. they/study Spanish/now
8. Peter/get up/now

6 Contrast the simple and present continuous verb forms.

Examples:	he/study/every day	*He studies every day.*
	he/study/now	*He is studying now.*

1. they/work/now
2. they/work/every day
3. she/cook/dinner/every day
4. she/cook/dinner/now
5. I/practice/English/every morning
6. I/practice/English/now
7. he/get up/at 7:00/every day
8. he/get up/at 7:00/now
9. she/watch/television/now
10. they/watch/television/now
11. he/watch/television/every night
12. I/ ? / now
13. I/ ? / every day
14. you/ ? / now
15. you/ ? / every day

TRANSFORMATION DRILLS

1 Change *he* (third person singular) to *they* (third person plural).

Examples:	He	He works every day.
	They	*They work every day.*
	He	He usually gets up at seven o'clock.
	They	*They usually get up at seven o'clock.*

1. He goes to school at eight-thirty every morning.
2. He eats breakfast at home every morning.
3. He needs some food.
4. He has a lot of books.
5. He knows that girl.
6. He wants a new car.
7. He has a big black car.
8. He watches television every evening.
9. He does his homework every night.
10. He eats lunch at school every day.
11. He often visits his friends.
12. He usually studies in the evening.
13. He usually listens to music after school in the afternoon.
14. He works in the Centerville Post Office.
15. He does his work every day.

2 Change *every day* **to** *now*. **Change the simple verb to the present continuous form.**

Examples:	Simple verb form	He works every day.
	Present continuous	*He is working now.*
	Simple verb form	I study English every day.
	Present continuous	*I am studying English now.*

1. We study every day.
2. I speak English every day.
3. Peter gets up every morning.
4. He goes to school every morning.
5. Mr. Baker works in the garage every day.
6. Mrs. Baker cooks dinner for her family every day.
7. Mrs. Hill cleans her house every day.
8. I study my lessons every day.
9. Peter and Jerry study Spanish every day.
10. I listen to music every afternoon.
11. Mrs. Baker goes to the supermarket every Saturday.
12. She buys the food for her family.
13. Mr. Baker drives Mrs. Baker to the supermarket.
14. Mrs. Baker writes everything down on a piece of paper.
15. Peter's friends go to school every weekday.
16. I do drills every day.
17. We study and practice English grammar every day.
18. They go home every afternoon.
19. Mr. and Mrs. Baker live in Centerville with their children.
20. You listen to our sentences every day.

3 Change *now* **to** *every day*. **Change the present continuous verb form to the simple form.**

| Examples: | Present continuous | He is working now. |
| | Simple verb form | *He works every day.* |

1. I am speaking English now.
2. She is cooking dinner now.
3. Mrs. Carter is teaching English now.
4. Mr. Hill is working in the Post Office now.
5. Jerry's sister is studying now.
6. Peter's brother is playing the guitar now.
7. His mother and father are watching television now.
8. My sister is working now.
9. Peter is listening to music now.
10. We are practicing English now.
11. I am speaking English now.
12. You are teaching English in this school now.
13. Mrs. Carter's daughter is sleeping now.
14. Her aunt is cleaning the living room now.
15. Her cousins are attending classes now.
16. Peter is taking a bath now.

4 **Add tag questions to these statements.**

Examples: Statement   He works every day.
          + Tag question   *He works every day, doesn't he?*

          Statement   He is studying now.
          + Tag question   *He is studying now, isn't he?*

1. She is cooking now, _____?
2. She cooks every day, _____?
3. You are teaching now, _____?
4. You teach every day, _____?
5. Peter studies every day, _____?
6. Joan works every day, _____?
7. She is working now, _____?
8. Carol and Linda go to school every day, _____?
9. They are eating, _____?
10. He has some brown shoes, _____?
11. Mrs. Baker needs some coffee, _____?
12. You are speaking English, _____?

13. I have a good book, _____?
14. Peter gets up at seven o'clock, _____?
15. Your brother is an auto mechanic, _____?
16. He works in a garage, _____?
17. English is a difficult language, _____?
18. Peter has blond hair and blue eyes, _____?
19. His father has brown hair and brown eyes, _____?
20. This is number twenty, _____?

WRITING PRACTICE

Choose one word for each blank space.

Peter Baker is a (1)_____ in the Centerville High School. Every weekday he does about the same things. He (2)_____ up, dresses, eats (3)_____, and goes to school every morning. He attends (4)_____ in school every day. Every afternoon he (5)_____ home and listens to music. Every evening he (6)_____ dinner with his family and watches (7)_____ for an hour or two. Then he does his homework. After that he takes a (8)_____ . Then he goes to bed.

SITUATIONAL PRACTICE

1 Pick up one of the picture cards for this lesson and ask other students various questions about the picture.

2 Give a short speech. Tell the class about what you do every day. Also tell them the time that you do the things you do.

3 Ask students what time they do things. For example:

"What time do you get up?"
"What time do you eat breakfast?"
"What time do you go to school?"
(*Continue.*)

4 Ask four or five students to come to the front of the room. Ask each student to tell what time he does a certain thing. Then ask other students questions such as:

"What time does John get up?"
"What time does Ruth get up?"
"What time does José get up?"
(*Continue.*)

After the students answer the questions, ask other students to come to the front of the room and repeat the procedure using a different question.

5 Contrast the simple and present continuous verb forms by asking pairs of questions such as:

"Do you get up every day?"   (Yes, I do.)
"Are you getting up now?"   (No, I'm not.)
"Are you eating lunch now?"   (No, I'm not.)
"Do you eat lunch every day?"   (Yes, I do.)
(*Continue.*)

Lesson Eleven

Mr. Anderson

LISTENING DRILL

Beginning with this lesson you will practice hearing the difference between various English consonants.

Step 1. Listen to your teacher pronounce the words below several times.
Step 2. Listen to your teacher say each word and decide if it is number 1, 2, 3, 4, or 5.
Step 3. Answer with the number when the teacher pronounces the words.

1	2	3	4	5
tin	sin	thin	shin	chin

READING

Mrs. Baker has one brother. His name is Sam Anderson. Mr. Anderson is a farmer. He lives in the country. He has a farm. It is a big farm, and the land is good, so Mr. Anderson and his family have a good life there.

Mr. Anderson is a healthy man. He is big and he has a lot of strength. He has a lot of land and a lot of animals. He has a lot of children, too.

Mr. Anderson doesn't have some of the things that many people in the city have. He owes money to the bank for his farm. He pays the bank a lot of money every month so he doesn't have much money to buy things with. He has worked hard all his life. He didn't have time to go to school very much and he doesn't have much education. He doesn't like to read books very much, but he knows a lot about farms and animals. The Andersons don't have many neighbors. It's very quiet on the farm, and everybody sleeps well at night.

Mr. Anderson's farm is about 50 miles from the Bakers' home. Sometimes the Bakers visit the Andersons on the weekend, and in the summer Peter and Tom go and work on their uncle's farm.

In this lesson we are going to talk about Mr. Anderson and his family. We are going to talk about the things he has and the things he doesn't have.

"YES OR NO" QUESTIONS

Give short answers.

1. Is Mr. Anderson Mrs. Hill's brother?
2. Is Mr. Anderson Mrs. Baker's brother?
3. Does Mr. Anderson live in the country?
4. Does Mr. Anderson live in Centerville?
5. Does Mr. Anderson have a lot of money?

"TAG" QUESTIONS

Give short answers.

1. Mr. Anderson is a farmer, isn't he?
2. He has a big family, doesn't he?
3. He doesn't live in Centerville, does he?
4. He has a lot of money, doesn't he?
5. He has a lot of education, doesn't he?

6. He knows a lot about farms and animals, doesn't he?

7. Peter and Tom are Mr. Anderson's nephews, aren't they?

8. You understand this story, don't you?

CONVERSATIONS

1   A. Mr. Anderson is a farmer, isn't he?
    B. Yes, he is. He lives in the country.
    A. Does he have much money?
    B. No, he doesn't. He has a lot of land, but he doesn't have much money.
    A. He has a lot of children, doesn't he?
    B. Yes, he does. He has six children and his wife is expecting another one soon.

2   A. Who is Mr. Anderson?
    B. He is Mrs. Baker's brother.
    A. Oh, then he is Peter's uncle, isn't he?
    B. Yes, that's right.
    A. Do the Bakers often visit Mr. Anderson?
    B. Not very often, but they sometimes drive to the Andersons' farm on the weekends.

3   A. What do Peter and Tom do in the summer?
    B. They usually go to their uncle's farm.
    A. What do they do on the farm?
    B. They work hard for their uncle.
    A. That is good for them, isn't it?
    B. Yes, it is. They have a healthy life on the farm, and they make a little money.

GRAMMAR NOTES

1. COUNT AND NON-COUNT NOUNS (Continued)

In Lesson Nine you learned that some nouns can be counted and others cannot. Words that can be counted have both singular and plural forms. Words that cannot be counted do not ordinarily have singular and plural forms. In this lesson we practice with these count and non-count nouns:

COUNT		NON-COUNT
child	children	strength
animal	animals	education
book	books	land
neighbor	neighbors	money

Notice that *money* is a non-count noun. We can count *dollars* or *cents*, but we do not ordinarily use *money* as a count noun.

2. MANY AND MUCH

The words *many* and *much* often come before nouns. They indicate a large quantity. *Many* is used with count nouns. *Much* is used with non-count nouns.

COUNT	NON-COUNT
many children	much strength
many animals	much education
many books	much land
many neighbors	much money

We often use *much* and *many* in questions:

Does he have many children?
Do you have much money?
Do they have many neighbors?

We also use *much* and *many* in negative statements:

He doesn't have many neighbors.
I don't have much time.
They don't have many children.

Note: *We do not often use* many *in affirmative statements. We almost never use* much *in affirmative statements.*

In conversation, it is common to use *a lot of* in place of *much* and *many* in affirmative statements.

3. *A LOT OF*

The expression *a lot of* is commonly used in ordinary conversation to indicate a large quantity. In formal writing other expressions such as *a large amount* or *a large quantity* are considered to be better style.

A lot of may be used with both count and non-count nouns. It may be substituted for either *much* or *many.*

COUNT	NON-COUNT
a lot of children	a lot of land
a lot of books	a lot of education
a lot of animals	a lot of money
a lot of neighbors	a lot of strength

A lot of may be used in affirmative statements, negative statements, and questions.

AFFIRMATIVE STATEMENTS	NEGATIVE STATEMENTS
He has a lot of strength.	He doesn't have a lot of money.
He has a lot of children.	He doesn't have a lot of neighbors.
I have a lot of books.	I don't have a lot of money.

QUESTIONS

Does he have a lot of land?
Do you need a lot of coffee?
Do they want a lot of children?

Remember to use *a lot of* rather than *much* or *many* in affirmative statements in ordinary conversation.

4. A LOT OF

Although it is common to use *a lot of* in ordinary conversation, it is sometimes considered better to use other expressions in formal writing. Here are a few examples:

> He has *a great deal of* money.
> They sell *a large quantity of* clothes.
> He needs *a large quantity* of sugar.

It is not necessary to learn these expressions now. You will become familiar with them later as you learn more English.

5. MONTHS AND SEASONS

In most of North America there are four seasons; Spring, Summer, Fall (Autumn), and Winter. There are twelve months in a year. The months and seasons in North America correspond as follows:

SUMMER	SPRING
June	March
July	April
August	May
FALL	**WINTER**
September	December
October	January
November	February

The months are numbered as follows:

1. January	4. April	7. July	10. October
2. February	5. May	8. August	11. November
3. March	6. June	9. September	12. December

Mr. Anderson has:

Mr. Anderson doesn't have:

87

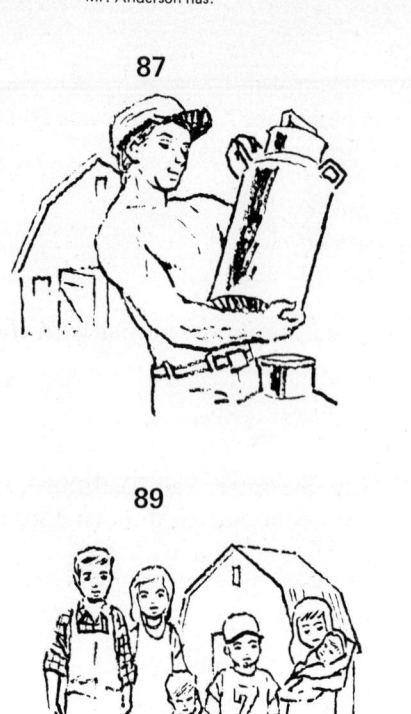

88

89

90

91

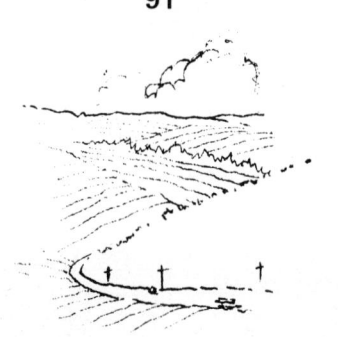

92

93

94

PICTURE DRILLS

1 Review the numbers 40 to 86.

2 Practice the numbers 87 to 94.

87. eighty-seven	91. ninety-one
88. eighty-eight	92. ninety-two
89. eighty-nine	93. ninety-three
90. ninety	94. ninety-four

3 Practice the nouns for the pictures.

strength	education
children	books
land	money
animals	neighbors

4 Count or non-count?

(The teacher will show the pictures and say the nouns. The students respond by telling if the nouns are count *or* non-count.*)*

TEACHER	STUDENTS
strength	non-count
education	non-count
children	count
books	count
(*Continue.*)	

5 Practice questions with *much* or *many*.

Use many *with count nouns. Use* much *with non-count nouns.*

1. Does Mr. Anderson have much strength?
2. Does Mr. Anderson have much education?
3. Does Mr. Anderson have many children?
4. Does Mr. Anderson have many books?
5. Does Mr. Anderson have much land?
   (*Continue.*)

6 Practice questions with *much* or *many* and short answers.

1. Does Mr. Anderson have much strength?	Yes, he does.
2. Does Mr. Anderson have much education?	No, he doesn't.
3. Does Mr. Anderson have many children?	Yes, he does.
4. Does Mr. Anderson have many books?	No, he doesn't.
(*Continue.*)	

7 Practice affirmative statements with *a lot of*.

(Use the odd-numbered pictures; 87, 89, 91, and 93)

Mr. Anderson has a lot of strength. He has a lot of land.
He has a lot of children. He has a lot of animals.

8 Practice negative statements with *much* or *many*.

(Use the even-numbered pictures; 88, 90, 92, and 94)

Mr. Anderson doesn't have much education. He doesn't have much money.
He doesn't have many books. He doesn't have many neighbors.

9 Practice a pattern of related statements. The first statement is affirmative and uses the expression *a lot of*. The second statement is negative and uses *much* or *many*.

87 & 88. Mr. Anderson has a lot of strength, but he doesn't have much education.

91 & 92. Mr. Anderson has a lot of land, but he doesn't have much money.

89 & 90. Mr. Anderson has a lot of children, but he doesn't have many books.

93 & 94. Mr. Anderson has a lot of animals, but he doesn't have many neighbors.

10 Repeat drill 11.9 having students pretend to be Mr. Anderson. Use as the subject: "I".

88 & 89. I am Sam Anderson. I am a farmer.
I have a lot of strength, but I don't have much education.
(Continue.)

11 Practice questions and answers with *a lot of*, *much*, or *many*.

1. Does Mr. Anderson have much strength?
    Yes, he has a lot of strength.
2. Does Mr. Anderson have much education?
    No, he doesn't have much education.
3. Does Mr. Anderson have many children?
    Yes, he has a lot of children.
  (Continue.)

SUBSTITUTION DRILLS

1 Practice the seasons of the year.

Example: What season is it?   (Spring)   *It is Spring.*

1. Spring   3. Fall
2. Summer   4. Winter

2 Practice the months of the year.

Example: What month is it? (January) *It is January.*

1. January 5. May 9. September
2. February 6. June 10. October
3. March 7. July 11. November
4. April 8. August 12. December

3 Practice the months with ordinal numbers.

Example: January/first *January is the first month of the year.*

1. January/first 7. July/seventh
2. February/second 8. August/eighth
3. March/third 9. September/ninth
4. April/fourth 10. October/tenth
5. May/fifth 11. November/eleventh
6. June/sixth 12. December/twelfth

4 Practice questions with count nouns and the word *many*.

Examples: he/children *Does he have many children?*
you/books *Do you have many books?*
Peter/friends *Does Peter have many friends?*

1. he/animals 11. his father/books
2. he/books 12. his uncle/neighbors
3. she/tomatoes 13. we/chairs
4. you/pencils 14. your sister/pictures
5. Mr. Baker/children 15. Mr. and Mrs. Baker/children
6. Mrs. Baker/dishes 16. you/animals
7. we/desks 17. this class/students
8. Mr. Hill/children 18. your friend/brothers
9. this school/rooms 19. his mother/dresses
10. your house/rooms 20. we/books

5 Practice questions with non-count nouns and the word *much*.

Examples: he/land *Does he have much land?*
she/coffee *Does she have much coffee?*
you/money *Do you have much money?*

1. he/land 9. Peter/strength
2. Mr. Baker/education 10. you strength
3. she/time 11. Joan/money
4. you/time 12. he/coffee
5. we/money 13. we/rice
6. they/bread 14. they/butter
7. Mr. Hill/education 15. Mrs. Baker/bread and butter
8. I/time 16. this class/time

6 Contrast using *many* and *much* with count and non-count nouns.

Examples: he/money   *Does he have much money?*
he/books   *Does he have many books?*
you/time   *Do you have much time?*
you/friends *Do you have many friends?*

1. he/land
2. he/animals
3. you/money
4. you/brothers
5. we/time
6. we/books
7. you/neighbors
8. you/money
9. Peter/education
10. Peter/strength
11. she/potatoes
12. she/rice
13. Joan/dresses
14. Joan/money
15. Mr. Anderson/money
16. Mr. Anderson/neighbors
17. they/food
18. they/bananas
19. they/butter
20. they/tomatoes

7 Practice affirmative statements with *a lot of*.

Examples: he/land   *He has a lot of land.*
he/books   *He has a lot of books.*
I/time   *I have a lot of time.*
I/classes   *I have a lot of classes.*

1. he/land
2. he/books
3. she/money
4. she/dresses
5. she/dishes
6. I/pans
7. I/clothes
8. Tom/shoes
9. Tom/white shirts
10. the teacher/red pencils
11. we/time
12. they/butter
13. they/potatoes
14. they/cheese
15. they/eggs
16. they/bread
17. they/milk
18. they/flour
19. I/good friends
20. English/words

TRANSFORMATION DRILLS

1 Change these statements from affirmative to negative. Change *a lot of* to *much* or *many*.

Examples: Affirmative He has a lot of books
Negative   *He doesn't have many books.*

Affirmative I have a lot of money.
Negative   *I don't have much money.*

1. He has a lot of land.
2. She has a lot of dresses.
3. Mr. Baker has a lot of animals.
4. The Andersons have a lot of neighbors.
5. I have a lot of pens.
6. Centerville has a lot of banks.
7. He needs a lot of paper.
8. I want a lot of coffee.
9. Peter needs a lot of books.
10. Carol has a lot of beautiful clothes.
11. The Hills have a lot of children.
12. This school has a lot of bad students.
13. Joan's office has a lot of secretaries.
14. Centerville has a lot of schools.
15. Peter and Tom have a lot of clothes.
16. This lesson has a lot of difficult words.

2 Add tag questions to these statements.

> Examples: Statement   He has a lot of books.
> + Tag question   *He has a lot of books, doesn't he?*
>
> Statement   Linda is a pretty girl.
> + Tag question   *Linda is a pretty girl, isn't she?*

1. He has a lot of money _____ ?
2. He gets up at seven o'clock, _____ ?
3. He is a farmer, _____ ?
4. They live in the country, _____ ?
5. She has some red shoes, _____ ?
6. Jerry is Mrs. Hill's son, _____ ?
7. Mr. and Mrs. Baker have four children, _____ ?
8. He often visits his friend, _____ ?
9. We are good students, _____ ?
10. This is a difficult class, _____ ?
11. Linda is a beautiful girl, _____ ?
12. Peter and Tom are brothers, _____ ?
13. You have a lot of time, _____ ?
14. This is number fourteen, _____ ?

3 Change the nouns to subject pronouns. Change the possessive nouns to possessive adjectives.

> Examples: Noun   *Jerry* is a student.
> Pronoun   *He is a student.*
>
> Possessive noun   *Jerry's* shoes are brown.
> Possessive adjective   *His shoes are brown.*

1. *Mr. Anderson* is a farmer.
2. *Mr. Anderson's* farm is big.
3. *Mrs. Anderson* has a lot of children.
4. *Peter* and *Tom* are *Mr. Anderson's* nephews.
5. *Jerry* has a lot of friends.
6. *Linda* is Jerry's sister.
7. *Joan* and *Carol* are pretty girls.
8. *Peter's* shoes are black.
9. *Linda's* eyes are brown.
10. *The Bakers'* house is big.
11. *The Andersons* live in the country.
12. *Sharon* is *Mrs. Carter's* daughter.

4 Change these statements to questions.

> Examples: Statement   He is a farmer.
> Question   *Is he a farmer?*
>
> Statement   He lives in the country.
> Question   *Does he live in the country?*

1. He has a lot of children.
2. They have some animals.
3. Peter does his homework every evening.
4. They watch television every evening.
5. You eat breakfast at 8:00 every morning.
6. Peter is a good student.
7. Carol and Linda are pretty girls.
8. Mrs. Baker has a lot of knives, forks, and spoons.
9. Mr. Baker needs some money.
10. They have a large old house.
11. Jerry wants a new red shirt.
12. Peter and Joan have blond hair and blue eyes.

13. Sharon is painting a picture now.
14. Mr. Hill has a lot of strength.
15. He is a strong man.

16. Mrs. Hill is cleaning the bedroom now.
17. She cleans the house every day.
18. We are practicing English sentences.

WRITING PRACTICE

Choose one word for each blank space.

Mr. Anderson is a farmer. He lives in the country. Mr. Anderson is a healthy (1)_____ . He is big and he has a lot (2)_____ strength. He has a lot of land and a (3)_____of animals. He (4)_____a lot of children, too.

Mr. Anderson doesn't (5)_____some of the things that many people in the city have. He owes (6)_____to the bank for his farm, so he doesn't have much money to (7)_____things with. He didn't have time to go to school very much, and he doesn't have much (8)_____.

SITUATIONAL PRACTICE

1 Say a month and ask other students to tell you what season it is (in North America).

Examples:	"June"	"Summer"
	"January"	"Winter"
	"September"	"Fall"
	(Continue.)	

2 Say the ordinal number of a month and have students tell its name.

Examples:	"First"	"January"
	"Fourth"	"April"
	"Ninth'	"September"
	(Continue.)	

3 Ask four students to come to the front of the room. Give a lot of books to one student, a lot of money (or other non-countable thing) to another, some other countable thing to the third, and some other non-countable thing to the fourth. Then ask a series of questions about who has what.

Does John have a lot of books?	Yes, he does.
Does Mary have many books?	No, she doesn't.
Does Tom have much money?	Yes, he does.
Does José have much money?	No, he doesn't.
(Continue.)	

You can ask the students who are holding the things questions, too.

Do you have many books?	Yes, I do.
Do you have much money?	No, I don't.
(Continue.)	

Ask questions with *who*.

Who has a lot of books?   John
Who has a lot of paper?   Mary
(*Continue.*)

4 Ask several students to pretend that they are various people in Centerville and their friends and relatives (the Bakers, the Hills, and the Andersons). Ask them questions.

What is your name?   What do you do every day?
Where do you live?   What are you doing now?
How old are you?   What color is your hair?
Are you a student?
(*Continue.*)

Lesson Twelve

LISTENING DRILL

Step 1. Listen to your teacher pronounce the words below several times.
Step 2. Listen to your teacher say each word and decide if it is number 1, 2, 3, 4, or 5.
Step 3. Answer with the number when the teacher pronounces the words.

1	2	3	4	5
see	tee	dee	thee	zee

READING

Linda Hill is Jerry Hill's sister. She lives in Centerville with her mother, father, brother, aunt, and cousin. Her father is a postman. He works in the Centerville post office. Her aunt is a teacher in the Centerville High School. Linda is fourteen years old. She has black hair and brown eyes. She is a pretty girl.

Linda likes parties and she is going to have a party next Saturday afternoon. She is going to invite a lot of guests. She is going to have a large party. Next Friday after school she is going to go to the supermarket. She is going to buy a lot of food for her party. She is going to buy a lot of soft drinks, a lot of candy, a lot of fruit, a lot of cake, a lot of cookies, and a lot of ice cream.

You remember Carol Baker, don't you? She is Peter Baker's sister. She lives in Centerville with her mother, father, sister, and two brothers. She is younger than Linda Hill. She is twelve years old. She has brown hair and brown eyes. She looks like her father.

Carol is going to have a party the week after next. It is going to be one week after Linda's party. Linda is going to have a large party, but Carol isn't. Carol is going to have a small party. She is going to invite only a few guests. Carol is going to go to the store on Saturday morning before her party. She is going to go with her mother. Carol is going to buy a few soft drinks, a little candy, a little fruit, a little cake, a few cookies, and a little ice cream.

"YES OR NO" QUESTIONS

Give the correct short answer.

1. Is Linda Jerry's sister?
2. Does Linda live in Centerville?
3. Is her father an auto mechanic?
4. Does Carol live in Centerville, too?
5. Is Linda going to have a party next week?
6. Is Carol going to have a party the week after next?
7. Is Linda going to have a large party?
8. Is Carol going to have a large party?
9. Is Linda going to buy a lot of food?
10. Is Carol going to buy a lot of food?

"QUESTION WORD" QUESTIONS

Answer with complete sentences.

1. Who is Jerry's sister?
2. Who is Peter's sister?
3. Where does Linda live?
4. Where does Carol live?
5. How old is Linda?
6. How old is Carol?
7. Who is going to have a large party?
8. Who is going to have a small party?
9. What is Linda going to buy?
10. What is Carol going to buy?

CONVERSATIONS

1   A. Are you going to go to Linda's party?
    B. Yes, I am. Are you?
    A. I don't know. Is she going to have a large party?
    B. Yes, she is going to invite a lot of guests.
    A. What is she going to serve?
    B. Oh, you know, soft drinks, candy, fruit, ice cream, and so on.
    A. That sounds good. I think I'll go.

2   A. Carol is going to have a party, too, isn't she?
    B. Yes, she is. Are you going to go?
    A. I don't know. When is it going to be?
    B. The week after next on Saturday afternoon.
    A. Is she going to have a large party or a small party?
    B. It is going to be small. She is going to invite only a few guests.
    A. Good. I like small parties. I think I'll go.

3   A. I'm going to have a party next week.
    B. That's nice.
    A. And I want you to come, please.
    B. Thank you. When is it going to be?
    A. Next Saturday afternoon about three o'clock.
    B. Good. I'll be there about three.
    A. Fine. I'm glad you can come.

GRAMMAR NOTES

1. COUNT & NON-COUNT NOUNS (Continued)

In this lesson we practice with six more nouns. Two of these are count nouns and four are non-count nouns:

COUNT		NON-COUNT
drink	drinks	candy
cooky	cookies	fruit
		cake
		ice-cream

Candy and *cake* are used sometimes as count nouns also. In this lesson we will practice using them only as non-count nouns. *Fruit,* which we might expect to be a count noun, is most commonly used as a non-count noun. It is occasionally used as a count noun also. We will practice using it as a non-count noun in this lesson.

2. A FEW & A LITTLE

Many and *much* indicate a large quantity. *A few* and *a little* indicate a small quantity. *A few* is used with count nouns. *A little* is used with non-count nouns.

COUNT	NON-COUNT
a few soft drinks	a little coffee
a few cookies	a little cake
a few potatoes	a little rice
a few books	a little money
a few houses	a little land

A few and *a little* can be used in any kind of sentence: affirmative or negative statements and questions.

3. TOMORROW, NEXT WEEK, NEXT MONTH, NEXT YEAR, etc.

English has several words for future time. Some of the most common ones are:

tomorrow	next Monday (Tuesday, Wednesday, Thursday, etc.)
tomorrow morning	next week
tomorrow afternoon	next month
tomorrow night	next year
the day after tomorrow	next January (February, March, April, etc.)
the week (month, year, etc.) after next	

These words indicate future time. They are generally used with a verb form that indicates future time or probability. They are often placed at the end of a sentence, but they can be placed at the beginning of the sentence or in other positions.

4. GOING TO

English often indicates future time, intention, or probability with the expression *going to. Going to* is used before the simple form of the verb. A form of *be* (*am, is, are*) is used as an auxiliary verb. It is important to remember that *going to* before a simple verb indicates future time. It does not have the same meaning as the verb *go. Going to* can be used before the verb *go* to indicate future time. Notice these examples:

STATEMENTS

I am going to study tomorrow.
She is going to have a party next week.
They are going to go the farm next summer.
Jerry is going to buy a new shirt tomorrow.
We are going to have a party.

QUESTIONS

Are you going to buy some food tomorrow?
Is she going to have a party next Saturday?
Is Peter going to go to the party?
Are they going to watch television tonight?
Is Linda going to have a large party?

NEGATIVE STATEMENTS

She isn't going to buy a lot of food tomorrow.
I'm not going to listen to music this afternoon.
We aren't going to swim next Friday.
Mr. Baker isn't going to work tomorrow.

TAG QUESTIONS

Carol is going to have a party, isn't she?
You are going to go to the party, aren't you?
We are going to study English next year, aren't we?
He is going to go home, isn't he?

English also uses the auxiliary *will* to express future time, probability, or intention. You will study this later.

5. *WHEN*

You have practiced five question words in English. In this lesson we introduce another—*when*. *When* is used to ask about time:

When are you going to go to the store?
    I'm going to go tomorrow morning.

When is she going to have the party?
    She is going to have it next Saturday.

When are you going to study this?
    I'm going to study it tonight.

Here are six question words. Listen to your teacher pronounce them and see if you can identify them by number:

1	2	3	4	5	6
who	what	when	where	how	which

When is used for any general time idea. Questions with *when* can be answered by time words such as *now, tomorrow, this afternoon,* etc. They can also be answered by words for clock time: *at two o'clock, at ten-thirty,* etc. If we want to be sure to have an answer with clock time, we often ask questions with the expression *What time.*

95

96

97

98

99

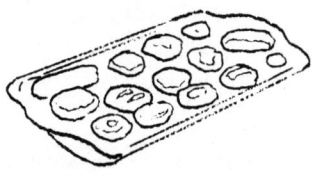

100

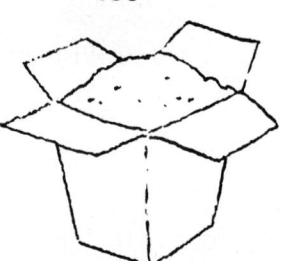

PICTURE DRILLS

1 Review the numbers from 1 to 94.

2 Practice the numbers from 95 to 100.

95. ninety-five	98. ninety-eight
96. ninety-six	99. ninety-nine
97. ninety-seven	100. one hundred

3 Practice the nouns for the picture in this lesson.

soft drinks	candy
fruit	cake
cookies	ice cream

4 Count or Non-count?

The teacher will say the words. The students respond by telling if the words are count *or* non-count.

TEACHER	STUDENTS
soft drinks	count
candy	non-count
fruit	non-count
cake	non-count
(*Continue.*)	

5 Practice statements with *going to* indicating future time and the verb *buy*.

1. She is going to buy soft drinks tomorrow.
2. She is going to buy candy tomorrow.
3. She is going to buy fruit tomorrow.
4. She is going to buy cake tomorrow.
   (*Continue.*)

6 Practice statements with *going to* indicating future time, and *a lot of* indicating a large quantity. Use the name *Linda*.

1. Linda is going to buy a lot of soft drinks tomorrow.
2. Linda is going to buy a lot of candy tomorrow.
3. Linda is going to buy a lot of fruit tomorrow.
   (*Continue.*)

7 Practice statements with *going to* and *a few* or *a little*.

Use a few *with count nouns. Use* a little *with non-count nouns. Use the name Carol.*

1. Carol is going to buy a few soft drinks tomorrow.
2. Carol is going to buy a little candy tomorrow.

3. Carol is going to buy a little fruit tomorrow.
4. Carol is going to buy a little cake tomorrow.
5. Carol is going to buy a few cookies tomorrow.
6. Carol is going to buy a little ice cream tomorrow.

8 Practice questions with *going to.*

1. Is she going to buy a lot of soft drinks?
2. Is she going to buy a lot of candy?
3. Is she going to buy a lot of fruit?
   (*Continue.*)

9 Practice questions with short answers. Use the names *Linda* and *Carol.*

1. Is Linda going to buy a lot of soft drinks?	Yes, she is.
2. Is Carol going to buy a lot of soft drinks?	No, she isn't.
3. Is Linda going to buy a lot of candy?	Yes, she is.
4. Is Carol going to buy a lot of candy?	No, she isn't.
(*Continue.*)	

10 Practice a pattern of questions with long answers.

1. Is Carol going to buy a lot of soft drinks?
      No, she isn't, but she is going to buy a few.

2. Is Carol going to buy a lot of candy?
      No, she isn't, but she is going to buy a little.

3. Is Carol going to buy a lot of fruit?
      No, she isn't, but she is going to buy a little.
   (*Continue.*)

11 Review statements with the present continuous verb form.

1. She is buying soft drinks now.
2. She is buying candy now.
3. She is buying fruit now.

12 Review statements with the simple verb form.

1. She buys soft drinks every Saturday.
2. She buys candy every Saturday.
3. She buys fruit every Saturday.
   (*Continue.*)

13 Contrast the three verb forms.

1. now	She is buying soft drinks now.
2. tomorrow	She is going to buy soft drinks tomorrow.
3. every Saturday	She buys soft drinks every Saturday.
4. now	She is buying candy now.
5. tomorrow	She is going to buy candy tomorrow.
6. every Saturday	She buys candy every Saturday.
7. now	She is buying fruit now.
(*Continue.*)	

14 When the teacher says the sentences, the students give the name of the verb form.

TEACHER	*STUDENTS*
She is buying soft drinks.	present continuous
She is going to buy soft drinks.	future
She buys soft drinks.	simple
She is going to buy soft drinks.	future
She is going to buy candy.	future
She is buying candy.	present continuous
(*Continue.*)	

SUBSTITUTION DRILLS

1 Practice affirmative statements with *going to* and words for future time.

> Examples: he/study/tomorrow
> > *He is going to study tomorrow.*
> > I/work/next Friday
> > *I am going to work next Friday.*
> > we/go home/tomorrow
> > *We are going to go home tomorrow.*

1. she/have a party/next week
2. she/buy coffee/tomorrow
3. I/study English/tomorrow
4. they/go to her party/next Saturday
5. she/work in the office/tomorrow
6. Mrs. Baker/cook dinner/this afternoon
7. Tom/study music/next year
8. I/go to the store/after school today
9. Peter and Jerry/talk to their friends/after school
10. we/have a party/next month
11. Peter/buy some new pants/next week
12. we/do the next exercise/in a few minutes

2 Practice questions with *going to*.

> Examples: he/study/tomorrow
> > *Is he going to study tomorrow?*
> > you/work/next Friday
> > *Are you going to work next Friday?*
> > we/go home/tomorrow
> > *Are we going to go home tomorrow?*

1. Carol/have a party/next week
2. you/go to her party/next week
3. Mr. Hill/work in the post office/tomorrow
4. Peter and Tom/go to their uncle's farm/next summer
5. you/buy some new pants/next Saturday
6. she/buy a few bananas/this afternoon
7. Mrs. Carter/teach English/next year
8. Sharon/go to school/next year
9. they/live in Centerville/next year
10. Linda/have a large party/next Saturday afternoon
11. she/go to the supermarket with her mother/next Saturday
12. we/do the next exercise/today

3 Practice negative statements with *going to*.

Examples:　he/work/tomorrow
　　　　　　　He isn't going to work tomorrow.
　　　　　I/go to school/tomorrow
　　　　　　　I'm not going to go to school tomorrow.
　　　　　we/study/next Sunday
　　　　　　　We aren't going to study next Sunday.

1. she/invite a lot of guests
2. I/go to school/next summer
3. we/buy any new books/tomorrow
4. Carol/buy much food/next week
5. Jerry/go to Carol's party/next Saturday afternoon
6. the Bakers/buy a new house/next year
7. Mr. Hill/work/next Saturday and Sunday
8. we/get up at 7:30/tomorrow morning
9. I/eat lunch at school/today
10. he/listen to music/this afternoon
11. Mr. and Mrs. Baker/buy a lot of new clothes/next month
12. Carol/buy many soft drinks for her party/the week after next

4 Practice statements in future time with *a little* or *a few*. Use *a few* with count nouns. Use *a little* with non-count nouns. Use the verb *buy*.

Examples:　she/cookies
　　　　　　　She is going to buy a few cookies.
　　　　　I/coffee
　　　　　　　I am going to buy a little coffee.
　　　　　you/books
　　　　　　　You are going to buy a few books.

1. she/soft drinks
2. she/coffee
3. I/coffee
4. he/shirts
5. she/cups and glasses
6. Jerry/ice cream
7. Peter/cookies
8. Carol/food
9. I/books
10. he/bread
11. Mrs. Baker/butter
12. they/dresses
13. Mrs. Hill/milk
14. I/food
15. I/fruit
16. she/fruit and cake

5 Contrast three verb forms.

Examples:　he/study/now　　　　*He is studying now.*
　　　　　he/study/every day　　*He studies every day.*
　　　　　he/study/tomorrow　　*He is going to study tomorrow.*

I/work/now	*I am working now.*
I/work/every day	*I work every day.*
I work/tomorrow	*I am going to work tomorrow.*

1. she/work/now
2. she/work/every day
3. she/work/tomorrow
4. I/listen to the teacher/now
5. I/listen to the teacher/every day
6. I/listen to the teacher/tomorrow
7. Tom/dance/now
8. Tom/dance/tomorrow night
9. Tom/dance/every Saturday night
10. we/speak English/every day
11. we/speak English/now
12. we/speak English/tomorrow
13. Peter and Jerry/swim/now
14. Peter and Jerry/swim/every Saturday afternoon
15. Peter and Jerry/swim/tomorrow afternoon
16. Mrs. Baker/go to the supermarket/every Saturday
17. Mrs. Baker/go to the supermarket/tomorrow
18. Mrs. Baker/go to the supermarket/now
19. Mr. Hill/work in the post office/now
20. Mr. Hill/work in the post office/every weekday
21. Mr. Hill/work in the post office/next Monday
22. Peter and Tom/visit their uncle's farm/now
23. Peter and Tom/visit their uncle's farm/every summer
24. Peter and Tom/visit their uncle's farm/next summer

TRANSFORMATION DRILLS

1 Change the verbs from simple to future form. Change *every day* to *tomorrow* or make other suitable changes in time words.

Examples:	Simple	*He works every day.*
	Future	*He is going to work tomorrow.*
	Simple	*You study English every day.*
	Future	*You are going to study English tomorrow.*

1. She cooks dinner every day.
2. Mr. Baker works every day.
3. He gets up at seven o'clock every morning.
4. We go to school every day.
5. Jerry goes to school every day.
6. Mrs. Baker buys food every Saturday.
7. I speak English every day.
8. You eat dinner at six-thirty every day.
9. Jerry and Peter listen to music every day.
10. Mrs. Carter teaches every day.
11. She cleans the house every day.
12. Joan types letters every day.
13. We do drills every day.
14. Peter eats lunch at school every day.
15. Linda reads every day.
16. Peter and Tom work on their uncle's farm every summer.

2 Change the verbs from present continuous to future form. Change *now* to *tomorrow*.

Examples:	Present continuous	*He is swimming now.*
	Future	*He is going to swim tomorrow.*
	Present continuous	*They are reading now.*
	Future	*They are gong to read tomorrow.*

1. She is buying a lot of food now.
2. Carol is buying a few cookies now.
3. Mr. Hill is watching television now.
4. Mrs. Baker is cooking dinner now.
5. Linda is having a party now.
6. We are practicing English now.

7. Carol is painting a picture now.
8. Tom is studying music now.
9. Mr. Baker is fixing a car now.
10. They are talking to their friends now.
11. Peter's sister is working now.
12. Mrs. Baker's husband is driving to the store now.
13. We are speaking English now.

14. The Bakers are visiting the Andersons now.
15. The old woman is cooking now.
16. The young woman is cleaning the living room now.
17. The tall boy is singing in church now.
18. Peter's father is fixing our car now.
19. His sister is cooking breakfast now.
20. His friends are having a party now.

3 Change these statements to questions. Notice that there are different verb forms.

Examples: Statement   She is going to have a party next week.
            Question   *Is she going to have a party next week?*

            Statement   She likes large parties.
            Question   *Does she like large parties?*

            Statement   She is buying food for the party now.
            Question   *Is she buying food for the party now?*

1. Linda is going to have a party next week.
2. She is going to have a large party.
3. She needs a lot of food.
4. She is going to buy the food tomorrow.
5. Linda has a lot of friends.
6. Carol is one of Linda's friends.
7. Jerry is Linda's brother.

8. This month is December.
9. Tom and Carol are going to dance at Linda's party.
10. The rich man is eating dinner now.
11. He eats dinner at seven o'clock every evening.
12. English is a difficult language.
13. Peter and Tom are Carol's brothers.

4 Add tag questions to the statements. Notice that there are different verb forms.

Examples: Carol is going to have a party, *isn't she?*
               She likes small parties, *doesn't she?*
               You are practicing English now, *aren't you?*

1. She is going to have a large party, _____ ?
2. She has a lot of friends, _____ ?
3. We have a large class, _____ ?
4. You need some coffee, _____ ?
5. Mrs. Baker is going to buy some bread, _____ ?
6. She is going to go to the store tomorrow, _____ ?
7. You are listening now, _____ ?
8. This month is January, _____ ?
9. Mr. Anderson is a farmer, _____ ?
10. Joan is a good secretary _____ ?
11. She has a lot of beautiful dresses, _____ ?
12. Jerry and Linda have black hair, _____ ?
13. We are going to have a party, _____ ?
14. You like this class, _____ ?
15. You understand this drill, _____ ?
16. You are speaking English now, _____ ?
17. This is number seventeen, _____ ?
18. Jerry's sister is going to have a large party next week, _____ ?

WRITING PRACTICE

Choose one word for each blank space.

Linda Hill is Jerry Hill's sister. She lives in Centerville with her father, (1)_____,
brother, aunt and cousin. Linda likes parties and she is going to have a party next Saturday
afternoon. She is (2)_____ to invite a lot of guests. She is going to (3)_____
a large party. Next Friday after school, she is going (4) _____ go to the supermarket. She is going to buy a (5) _____ of food for her party. She is going to
(6) _____ a lot of soft drinks, a lot of candy, a lot (7) _____ cake,
a lot of cookies and a (8) _____ of ice cream.

SITUATIONAL PRACTICE

1 See which students in your class can name the seven days of the week, the twelve months of
the year, and the four seasons of the year.

2 See who can count from 1 to 25, from 26 to 50, from 51 to 75, and from 76 to 100.

3 Ask other students questions with *what time* and *tomorrow*. Use the future verb form. For
example:

"What time are you going to get up tomorrow?"
  "I'm going to get up at seven o'clock."

"What time are you going to eat breakfast tomorrow?"
  "I'm going to eat breakfast at seven thirty."
(*Continue.*)

4 Ask several students to come to the front of the room. Ask them questions about what they
are going to do next Saturday. Then ask other students questions about the students in the front
of the room. Be sure to use the future form, *going to*, in your questions and answers.

5 Contrast the verb forms that you have studied so far. Give students a time word (*now, every
day, tomorrow,*) and have them make up sentences using the correct verb form.

6 Use the picture cards from lesson ten (numbers 77 through 86) and contrast the three verb
forms:

now	He is getting up now.
every day	He gets up every day.
tomorrow	He is going to get up tomorrow.
(*Continue.*)	

7 Contrast the three verb forms by asking students questions about their own lives. Try to pick
questions that will have "yes" answers with some time words and "no" answers with other time
words:

Do you eat breakfast every day?	Yes, I do.
Are you eating breakfast now?	No, I'm not.
Are you going to eat breakfast tomorrow?	Yes, I am.
(*Continue.*)	

8 Review all the material that has been covered in Lessons One through Twelve by practicing questions and answers with picture cards 1 through 100.

9 Ask students various questions about Centerville, the Bakers, the Hills, and the Andersons.

Lesson Thirteen

What Are They Going to Be?

LISTENING DRILL

Step 1. Listen to your teacher pronounce the words below several times.
Step 2. Listen to your teacher say each word and decide if it is number 1, 2, 3, 4, or 5.
Step 3. Answer with the number when the teacher pronounces the words.

1	2	3	4	5
dag	jag	rag	wag	zag

READING

What do you remember about the Bakers? They live in Centerville, of course. Mr. Baker is an auto mechanic and Mrs. Baker is a housewife. They have four children. The children's names are Joan, Peter, Tom, and Carol. Joan is a secretary. She works in an office. Peter, Tom, and Carol are students. They go to school every day.

Peter, Tom, and Carol all have plans for the future after they finish high school. Peter is going to study engineering. He is going to be an engineer. Tom loves music and likes to play the guitar. He is going to study music. He is going to be a musician. Carol likes to paint and draw pictures. She is going to study art. She is going to be an artist.

Jerry and Linda Hill have plans for the future, too. Jerry is going to study law. He is going to be a lawyer. Linda likes people and wants to help them. She is going to study nursing. She is going to be a nurse.

You remember Sharon Carter, too, don't you? She is Jerry and Linda's cousin. Her mother is a teacher in the Centerville High School. Sharon is just a small girl. She is five years old. She doesn't really have plans for the future, but she has dreams. She says she is going to study acting and be an actress. Maybe she will. Who knows?

"YES OR NO" QUESTIONS

Give the correct short answer.

1. Do the Bakers live in Centerville?
2. Is Mr. Baker an auto mechanic?
3. Is Mrs. Baker a teacher?
4. Is Joan Baker a secretary?
5. Do Peter, Tom, and Carol go to school every day?

"TAG" QUESTIONS

Give the correct short answer.

1. Peter, Tom, and Carol have plans for the future, don't they?
2. Peter is going to study engineering, isn't he?
3. Peter is going to be an engineer, isn't he?
4. Carol is going to study nursing, isn't she?
5. Carol is going to be a nurse, isn't she?

"QUESTION WORD" QUESTIONS
Answer with complete sentences.

1. What is Peter going to study? What is he going to be?
2. What is Tom going to study? What is he going to be?
3. What is Carol going to study? What is she going to be?
4. What is Jerry going to study? What is he going to be?
5. What is Linda going to study? What is she going to be?
6. Where do the Bakers live?
7. How old is Peter Baker?
8. When is Peter going to study engineering?

CONVERSATIONS

1   A. Peter and Jerry are in high school, aren't they?
     B. Yes, they're both in high school now.
     A. What are they going to do after they finish high school?
     B. Peter is going to study engineering.
     A. And what about Jerry?
     B. He is going to study law. He is going to be a lawyer.

2   A. Tom plays the guitar, doesn't he?
     B. Yes, he plays very well.
     A. Is he going to study music after he finishes high school?
     B. Yes, he is. He is going to be a musician.
     A. That is a difficult life, isn't it?
     B. Yes, sometimes it is difficult, but Tom loves music and that is what he wants to do.

3   A. You're a student in this school, aren't you?
     B. Yes, I am. I'm studying English.
     A. What are you going to do after you learn English?
     B. I'm not sure. I'm going to think about that for awhile.
     A. That's a good idea. It is a very important decision.
     B. Yes, it is. What are you planning to do?
     A. I'm thinking about it, too.

GRAMMAR NOTES

1. ENGINEERING, NURSING, ACTING

Not all words that end in -ing function as verbs. In this lesson we practice these patterns:

Peter is going to study *engineering*.
Jerry is going to study *law*.
Linda is going to study *nursing*.
Tom is going to study *music*.
Carol is going to study *art*.
Sharon is going to study *acting*.

The underlined words all function as nouns. They are the objects of the verb *study*. Many other words that end in -ing function as nouns.

2. *GOING TO BE*

Going to be is the future form of the linking verbs (*am*, *is*, and *are*). Notice these examples.

LINKING VERB PRESENT	LINKING VERB FUTURE
He is a lawyer.	He is going to be a lawyer.
She is a nurse.	She is going to be a nurse.
I am an artist.	I am going to be an artist.
She is happy.	She is going to be happy.
He is tall.	He is going to be tall.
Joan is here.	Joan is going to be here.
They are downtown.	They are going to be downtown.

3. SUBJECTS AND OCCUPATIONS

In this lesson we practice with pairs of related words. One of the pair refers to a subject of study. The other word of the pair refers to the occupation of a person who has studied the subject and works with it. Notice these examples.

SUBJECT OF STUDY	OCCUPATION
engineering	an engineer
law	a lawyer
nursing	a nurse
art	an artist
music	a musician
acting	an actress (or actor)

The subjects of study are non-count nouns. They do not have singular and plural forms and they are not preceded by *a* or *an*.

The occupations are count nouns. They have singular and plural forms and may be preceded by *a* or *an*.

4. WHY

In this lesson we practice with the question word *why*. *Why* asks the reason for, purpose of, or cause of some action or state. A question with *why* is often answered by a statement with the word *because*.

Why is he going to study engineering?
Because he wants to be an engineer.

Why are you studying English?
Because I want to go to a university in the United States.

Why is she going to the store?
Because she needs some food.

We have practiced with seven question words now. See if you can distinguish between the words when the teacher pronounces them.

1	2	3	4	5	6	7
who	what	when	where	why	how	which

5. THE SCHOOL SYSTEM IN THE UNITED STATES

The school system differs a little bit from one part of the country to another, but perhaps the most common system is as follows.

Primary School (also called Grade School)	Kindergarden and grades 1 through 6
Junior High School	Grades 7, 8, and 9
High School	Grades 10, 11, and 12

Many students who finish high school go on to a trade or technical school or a college or university. It generally takes four years in a college or university to obtain a bachelor's degree. Some students continue to study in graduate schools and obtain graduate degrees.

6. ACTOR AND ACTRESS

A person who performs on the stage or in movies is called an actor or actress. A man is called an *actor*. A woman is called an *actress*.

There are several other names of occupations that change form for male or female. The ending *-ess* frequently indicates that the person referred to is female.

7. ASKING ABOUT OCCUPATIONS

People in the United States often ask about occupations, using the question "What do you do?" or "What does he do?", "What does she do?", etc. Notice these examples:

What do you do?
I'm a student.

What does she do?
She's a teacher.

What does he do?
He's an engineer.

The question "What is your occupation?" is rather formal. It may be used in a formal situation but is not common in ordinary conversation.

101

ENGINEERING
ENGINEER

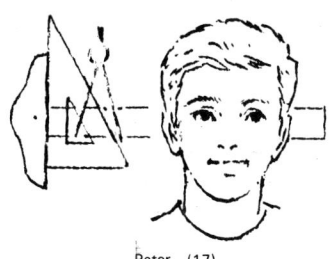

Peter (17)

102

LAW
LAWYER

Jerry (17)

103

NURSING
NURSE

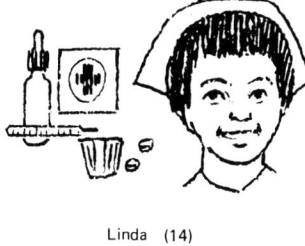

Linda (14)

104

MUSIC
MUSICIAN

Tom (16)

105

ART
ARTIST

Carol (12)

106

ACTING
ACTRESS

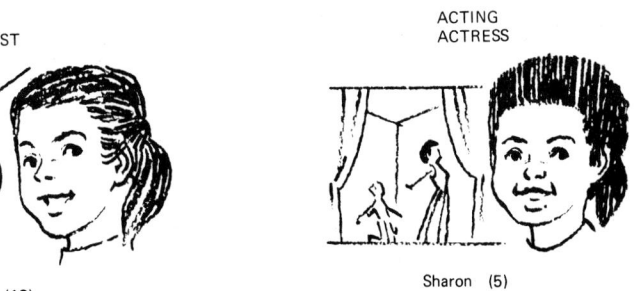

Sharon (5)

PICTURE DRILLS

1 Practice the numbers from 101 to 106.

101. one hundred and one   104. one hundred and four
102. one hundred and two   105. one hundred and five
103. one hundred and three   106. one hundred and six

2 Review possessive adjectives

1. What is his name?   His name is Peter.
2. What is his name?   His name is Jerry.
3. What is her name?   Her name is Linda.
4. What are their names?   Their names are Tom and Carol.
   (*Continue.*)

3 Review patterns for telling age.

1. How old is Peter?   He is seventeen years old.
2. How old is Jerry?   He is seventeen years old.
3. How old is Linda?   She is fourteen years old.
   (*Continue.*)

4 Practice the words for subjects of study.

engineering   law
nursing   music
art   acting

5 Practice future time statements with the subjects of study.

1. Peter is going to study engineering.   4. Tom is going to study music.
2. Jerry is going to study law.   5. Carol is going to study art.
3. Linda is going to study nursing.   6. Sharon is going to study acting.

6 Practice the words for occupations.

engineer   lawyer
nurse   musician
artist   actress

7 Practice future time statements with the occupations.

1. Peter is going to be an engineer.   4. Tom is going to be a musician.
2. Jerry is going to be a doctor.   5. Carol is going to be an artist.
3. Linda is going to be a nurse.   6. Sharon is going to be an actress.

8 Subject or Occupation?

The teacher pronounces a word. The students respond by telling if the word represents a subject of study or an occupation.

TEACHER	STUDENTS
engineering	subject
engineer	occupation
lawyer	occupation
law	subject
(*Continue.*)	

9 Contrast subjects of study and occupations with *going to study* and *going to be*.

What is Peter going to study?	He is going to study engineering.
What is Peter going to be?	He is going to be an engineer.
What is Jerry going to study?	He is going to study law.
What is Jerry going to be?	He is going to be a lawyer.
(*Continue.*)	

10 Practice questions with *why* and answers with *because*.

Why is Peter going to study engineering?
Because he is going to be an engineer.

Why is Jerry going to study law?
Because he is going to be a lawyer.
(*Continue.*)

11 Summary Drill.   Practice various question and answer patterns with the pictures.

Who is he?	He is Peter Baker.
What is his first name?	His first name is Peter.
What is his last name?	His last name is Baker.
Where does he live?	He lives in Centerville.
How old is he?	He is seventeen years old.
What color is his hair?	His hair is blond.
What color are his eyes?	His eyes are blue.
Does he go to high school?	Yes, he does.
What is he going to do after he finishes high school?	He is going to study engineering.
What is he going to be?	He is going to be an engineer.
(*Continue.*)	

SUBSTITUTION DRILLS

1 Practice *going to* with subjects of study.

Examples:	he/English	*He is going to study English.*
	I/art	*I am going to study art.*
	you/Chinese	*You are going to study Chinese.*

1. he/Spanish   2. I/English

3. she/art
4. he/engineering
5. Jerry/law
6. Linda/art
7. we/English

8. they/nursing
9. she/typing
10. Sharon/acting
11. Tom/music
12. I/?

2 Practice *going to be* **with occupations.**

Examples: he/teacher   *He is going to be a teacher.*
              I/engineer   *I am going to be an engineer.*
              you/musician   *You are going to be a musician.*

1. Jerry/lawyer
2. he/mechanic
3. she/secretary
4. you/musician
5. Carol/artist
6. she/housewife
7. Tom/musician
8. he/teacher

9. she/English teacher
10. he/postman
11. Peter/engineer
12. Sharon/actress
13. he/good lawyer
14. she/good wife
15. he/intelligent teacher
16. I/?

3 Contrast the use of *going to study* **with subjects of study and** *going to be* **with names of occupations.**

Examples: he/art   *He is going to study art.*
              he/artist   *He is going to be an artist.*

              I/nurse   *I am going to be a nurse.*
              I/nursing   *I am going to study nursing.*

1. she/acting
2. she/actress
3. he/law
4. he/lawyer
5. Peter/engineer
6. Peter/engineering
7. Tom/musician
8. Tom/music
9. she/nurse
10. she/nursing
11. I/English
12. I/teacher

13. she/typing
14. she/secretary
15. he/auto mechanic
16. they/artists
17. they/art
18. he/acting
19. he/actor
20. Jerry/law
21. Jerry/lawyer
22. my friend/Spanish
23. my friend/teacher
24. I/?

4 Practice using *going to be* **before adjectives.**

Examples: she/happy   *She is going to be happy.*
              he/strong   *He is going to be strong.*

1. he/happy
2. Peter/tall

3. I/happy
4. she/sick

5. she/healthy   8. he/short
6. he/big   9. he/old
7. she/beautiful   10. you/happy

5 Review and contrast three verb forms in statements.

Examples: he/study/now   *He is studying now.*
             he/study/every day   *He studies every day.*
             he/study/tomorrow   *He is going to study tomorrow.*

1. she/study art/now   7. I/go home/now
2. she/study art/every day   8. I/go home/every afternoon
3. she/study art/tomorrow   9. I/go home/next week
4. Peter/go to school/now   10. we/speak English/now
5. Peter/go to school/every day 11. we/speak English/every day
6. Peter/go to school/tomorrow 12. we/speak English/tomorrow

6 Review and contrast the three verb forms in questions.

Examples: he/study/now   *Is he studying now?*
             he/study/every day   *Does he study every day?*
             he/study/tomorrow   *Is he going to study tomorrow?*

1. you/work/now   7. Joan/type letters/now
2. you/work/every day   8. Joan/type letters/every day
3. you/work/tomorrow   9. Joan/type letters/tomorrow
4. Mrs. Baker/cook/now   10. we/do drills/now
5. Mrs. Baker/cook/every day   11. we/do drills/every day
6. Mrs. Baker/cook/tomorrow   12. we/do drills/tomorrow

7 Review *a few* with count nouns and *a little* with non-count nouns.

Examples: she/coffee   *She is going to buy a little coffee.*
             she/cookies   *She is going to buy a few cookies.*

1. he/shirts   9. I/pencils
2. he/coffee   10. he/pens
3. Carol/soft drinks   11. the school/desks
4. Carol/cake   12. Mrs. Hill/milk
5. I/bread   13. Carol/ice cream
6. we/butter   14. she/fruit
7. Tom/bananas   15. I/fruit
8. Mrs. Baker/food   16. I/eggs

TRANSFORMATION DRILLS

1 Review and practice the position of adjectives. Make one sentence by combining the two sentences given.

Examples: A)   He is going to be a lawyer.
             B)   He is going to be good.
             A+B) *He is going to be a good lawyer.*

A)   She is a woman.
B)   She is beautiful.
A+B)   *She is a beautiful woman.*

1. A)   She is going to be a wife.
   B)   She is going to be good.

2. A)   He is going to be a man.
   B)   He is going to be tall.

3. A)   They are going to be teachers.
   B)   They are going to be intelligent.

4. A)   He is a man.
   B)   He is old.

5. A)   Mr. Anderson is a man.
   B)   Mr. Anderson is strong.

6. A)   Mr. Baker is an auto mechanic.
   B)   Mr. Baker is very good.

7. A)   Joan is a secretary.
   B)   Joan is good.

8. A)   Jerry is going to be a man.
   B)   Jerry is going to be handsome.

9. A)   I am a student.
   B)   I am good.

10. A) English is a language.
    B) English is difficult.

11. A) Linda is a girl.
    B) Linda is pretty.

12. A) She is going to be a woman.
    B) She is going to be beautiful.

13. A) He is going to be a man.
    B) He is going to be rich.

14. A) These are drills.
    B) These are easy.

2 Change these statements to questions.

Examples: Statement   He is going to be a musician.
             Question   *Is he going to be a musician?*

             Statement   He has a guitar.
             Question   *Does he have a guitar?*

1. He is a student.
2. He is going to finish high school next year.
3. He goes to school every day.
4. She needs some coffee.
5. She has some money.
6. Peter is going to be an engineer.
7. He is going to study engineering.
8. He is usually a good student.
9. Carol is going to buy a few cookies.
10. She is going to buy a little fruit, too.
11. Jerry is tall.
12. He is a tall boy.
13. He is going to be a handsome man.
14. He wants to be a lawyer.
15. His father is a postman.
16. Mr. Anderson has a lot of land.
17. He has a lot of animals, too.
18. His wife is expecting another child soon.

3 Change these statements to questions beginning with the question word *why*.

Examples: Statement   He is studying English.
             "Why" question *Why is he studying English?*

             Statement   She needs some money.
             "Why" question *Why does she need some money?*

1. She is studying art.
2. He needs some paper.
3. You are reading that book.
4. Peter is talking to Carol.
5. They are going to the bank.
6. She wants a husband.

7. Joan is working in an office.
8. We are practicing English.
9. You are doing that.
10. They are going to go downtown.
11. Mrs. Baker is going to the supermarket.
12. Linda is going to have a large party.
13. She is going to be happy.

14. We are studying English.
15. He is watching television.
16. English is difficult for you.
17. Tom likes music.
18. He wants to be a musician.
19. He is going to study music.
20. Sharon is going to study acting.

WRITING PRACTICE

Choose one word for each blank space.

Peter, Tom and Carol all have plans for the future after they finish high (1) _____ .
Peter is going to study engineering. He is going to (2) _____ an engineer. Tom
loves music and likes to play the guitar. He is going to (3) _____ music.
He is going to be a musician. Carol likes to paint and draw pictures. She is (4)_____
to study art. She is going to (5)_____ an artist.

Jerry and Linda Hill have plans for the future, too. Jerry is going to study (6)_____ .
He is going to be a lawyer. Linda liked people and wants to help them. She is going to study
nursing. She is going to be a (7) _____ .

Sharon is a little girl. She is just five years old. She doesn't really have plans for the future,
but she has dreams. She says that she is going to study acting and be an (8) _____
someday.

SITUATIONAL PRACTICE

1 Ask students questions about their plans for the future. Use the expressions *going to study* or
going to be. Then ask other students questions about their classmates. See who can remember the
plans of their classmates.

2 Have students come to the front of the room and give short talks telling the class about what
they are doing now, and what they plan to do in the future.

3 Ask students about their brothers and sisters. Ask what they are doing now, and what they
plan to do in the future.

4 Have six students come to the front of the room. Have each student pretend to be one of the
people in the picture chart for this lesson. (You may give each of them a picture card to hold up
where everyone in the class can see it.)

Ask the students all the various question patterns that have been practiced in Lessons One through
Thirteen and have them answer using the pronoun "I". Have other students ask the questions also.

Ask other students in the class questions about the students in the front of the room who are
pretending to be people in the book.

5 Write a long sentence on the blackboard such as:

"Peter is going to walk to the store tomorrow afternoon because he needs some new shirts."

Then make up questions about the sentence using as many of the seven question words as have been introduced in the text. For example:

"Who is going to walk to the store?"
"Where is Peter going to walk?"
"When is Peter going to go to the store?"
"Why is he going to go to the store?"
"How is he going to go to the store?"
(*Continue.*)

Ask students to answer the questions first with short answers and then with complete sentences.

Then ask students to make up the questions. Give them the question word and tell them to make up a question.

Lesson Fourteen *Mr. Baker's Birthday*

LISTENING DRILL

1	2	3	4	5
lent	rent	went	vent	bent

READING

Next Friday is Mr. Baker's birthday. He is going to be 43 years old. Mrs. Baker and the children always give him presents on his birthday. They are going to have a party for him and give him presents next Friday. They are going to invite a few of his friends to the party.

What is everyone going to give him? Well, Mrs. Baker is going to buy some new shirts for him. Joan is making a new sweater for him. Peter is going to go downtown tomorrow and buy him a new radio. Tom doesn't have much money, but he wants to give his father a new watch. Joan is going to lend Tom some money to buy the watch. Carol doesn't have much money either, but she doesn't need any because she is painting a picture to give to her father. Mr. Baker's friends are going to give him presents, too, but we don't know what the presents are going to be.

Mrs. Baker is going to cook a good dinner and bake a birthday cake for Mr. Baker's party next Friday. Tom is going to play the guitar for everyone and Joan and Carol are going to sing for them. Everyone is going to have a wonderful time.

"YES OR NO" QUESTIONS

Give the correct short answer.

1. Is Mr. Baker going to be 45 years old next Friday?
2. Is he going to be 43 years old?
3. Are Mrs. Baker and the children going to have a party for him?
4. Is Joan making a sweater for Mr. Baker?
5. Is Peter going to give his father a book?
6. Does Tom want to give him a new watch?
7. Does Tom have a lot of money?
8. Is Joan going to lend some money to Tom?
9. Is Tom going to play the guitar for everyone at the party?
10. Are Joan and Carol going to sing for them?

"OR" QUESTIONS
Answer with full sentences.

1. Is Mr. Baker going to be 43 years old or 45 years old next Friday?
2. Is Mrs. Baker going to buy him some new shirts or new shoes?
3. Is Peter going to give him a new radio or a new watch?
4. Are they going to have a party for him next Friday or next Saturday?

"QUESTION WORD" QUESTIONS
Answer with full sentences.

1. Who is going to have a birthday next Friday?
2. How old is he going to be?
3. What is Joan making for him?
4. What is Peter going to give him?
5. Why is Joan going to lend Tom some money?
6. When are they going to have the birthday party?
7. Who is going to play the guitar at the party?
8. Who is going to sing?

CONVERSATIONS

1   (*Peter is talking to Carol.*)
   A. Next Friday is Dad's birthday, isn't it?
   B. Yes, he's going to be 43 years old.
   A. What are you going to buy for him?
   B. I'm not going to buy anything. I'm going to paint a picture for him.
   A. Good! He'll like that.

2   (*Peter is talking to Tom.*)
   A. What are we going to do for Dad's birthday party?
   B. Well, Mom is going to cook dinner and bake a cake.
   A. Are we going to invite a lot of guests?
   B. No, just a few of Dad's best friends.
   A. Are you going to play the guitar for the guests?
   B. Yes, and Joan and Carol are going to sing for them.

3   (*Two of Mr. Baker's friends are talking.*)
   A. Next Friday is Fred Baker's birthday, isn't it?
   B. Yes, it is. His family is going to have a party for him.
   A. Are you going to go to the party?
   B. Yes, I am. Are you going, too?
   A. Yes, I am. What are you going to give him?
   B. I don't know. I'm going to go downtown and buy something tomorrow.

GRAMMAR NOTES

1. OBJECT PRONOUNS

In previous lessons we have studied subject pronouns and a group of related words that we called possessive adjectives. In this lesson we practice with another group of related words that we call object pronouns. Here are the three groups of related words:

SUBJECT PRONOUNS	POSSESSIVE ADJECTIVES	OBJECT PRONOUNS
Singular	*Singular*	*Singular*
I	my	me
you	your	you
he	his	him
she	her	her
it	its	it
Plural	*Plural*	*Plural*
we	our	us
you	your	you
they	their	them

Object pronouns are used in several different ways. We will practice the most common uses in this lesson.

2. DIRECT OBJECTS

The primary object of a verb action is called the direct object of the verb. The person or thing that directly receives the action of the verb is the direct object. The direct object can be a noun or noun phrase or an object pronoun.

NOUN OBJECT	PRONOUN OBJECT
I know *John.*	I know *him.*
I see *Mary.*	I see *her.*
He is buying *a radio.*	He is buying *it.*
He likes *Peter and Jerry.*	He likes *them.*
I need *those cups.*	I need *them.*

3. INDIRECT OBJECT AFTER A PREPOSITION

Often the verb action has a secondary or indirect object.

Tom is going to play the guitar for the guests.

In the above sentence, *the guitar* is the direct object of the verb action and *the guests* are the indirect object. Both the direct and the indirect object can be changed to pronouns.

Tom is going to play it for them.

When the indirect object follows a preposition it is often called the object of the preposition. Here are some more examples.

INDIRECT NOUN OBJECT	INDIRECT PRONOUN OBJECT
She is making a shirt for *Tom.*	She is making a shirt for *him.*
He is lending money to *Linda.*	He is lending money to *her.*
Joan is singing for *the guests.*	Joan is singing for *them.*
She is cooking dinner for *Peter.*	She is cooking dinner for *him.*

4. TO & FOR

In this lesson we practice using indirect objects following the prepositions *to* and *for*. It is often difficult to understand which of the two prepositions should be used in certain cases. It is probably best for the beginning student to learn to associate certain verbs with *to* and other verbs with *for*.

VERBS WITH "TO"	*VERBS WITH "FOR"*
lend to	make for
give to	cook for
explain to	buy for
serve to	fix for
teach to	paint for
speak to	play for
say to	open for
	close for

In some cases one verb may be followed by either *to* or *for*. Then the meaning of the verb phrase is different when *for* is used and when *to* is used.

5. INDIRECT OBJECT FOLLOWING THE VERB

In many cases the indirect object may come between the verb and the direct object and no preposition is used. Notice these examples:

They always give him presents.   *him* is the indirect object. *presents* is the direct object.

Please give me some cake.   *me* is the indirect object. *cake* is the direct object.

Not all verbs can take an indirect object in this position and we will not drill this structure in this lesson. You will study it more later.

6. MOM & DAD

Mom and *Dad* are familiar forms of the more formal *Mother* and *Father*. *Mom* and *Dad* are often used by children talking to their own parents or when talking about the parents of their close friends.

7. COMMANDS AND REQUESTS

Commands and requests are often called *imperatives* in English grammar. They are usually made with the simple form of the verb and often have direct and indirect objects. An expression without any polite words such as *please* is a command. The use of *please* or a similar polite expression changes the command to a request.

COMMAND	*REQUEST*
Open the door for me!	Please open the door for me.
Give me a pencil!	Please give me a pencil.
Serve coffee to them!	Please serve coffee to them.
Buy a dress for her!	Please buy a dress for her.

We do not often give commands in ordinary daily life. It is always best to use *please* or a similar expression in order to be polite when making requests.

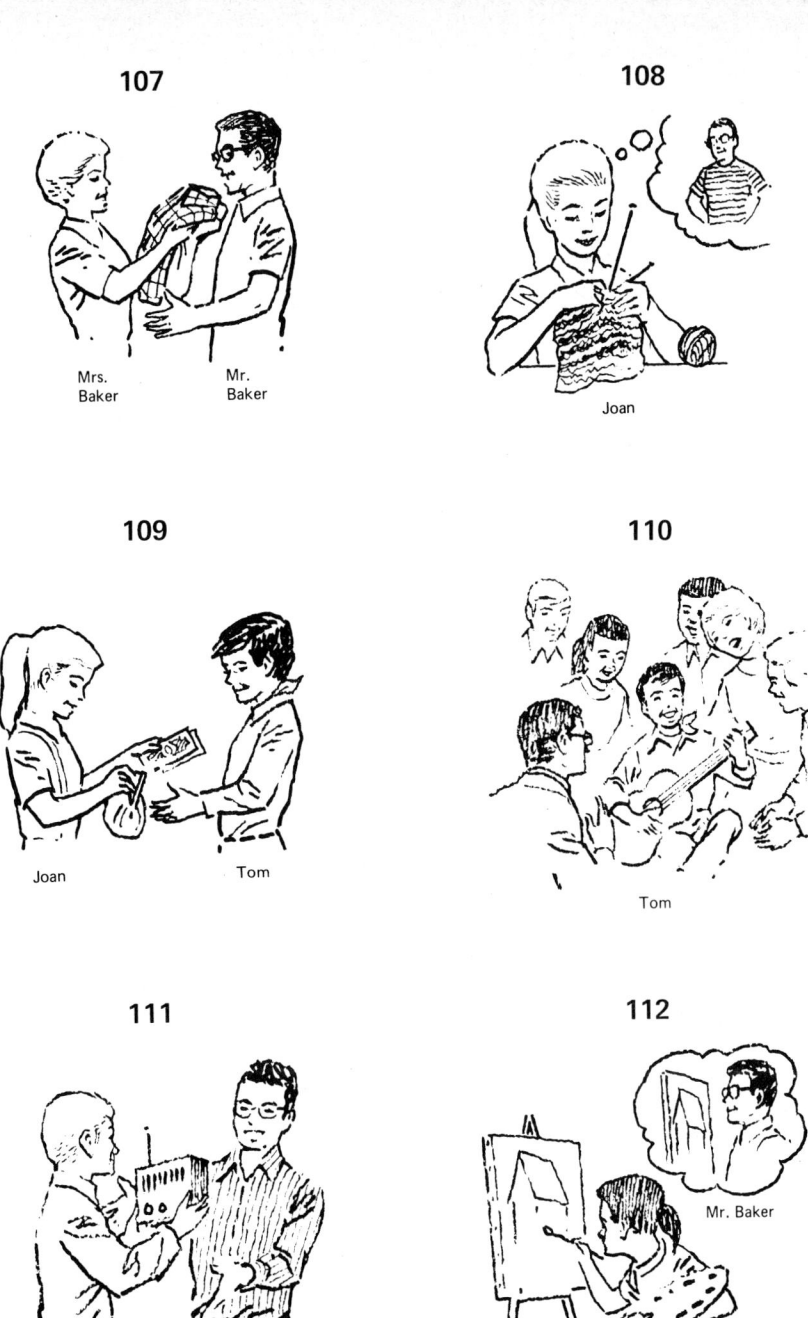

107

Mrs.
Baker

Mr.
Baker

108

Joan

109

Joan

Tom

110

Tom

111

Peter

Mr.
Baker

112

Mr. Baker

Carol

PICTURE DRILLS

1 Practice the numbers from 107 to 112.

107. one hundred and seven   110. one hundred and ten
108. one hundred and eight   111. one hundred and eleven
109. one hundred and nine   112. one hundred and twelve

2 Practice questions with direct noun objects.

1. Do you know Mrs. Baker?
2. Do you known Joan?
3. Do you know Tom?
4. Do you know Peter?
5. Do you know Carol?

3 Practice statements with direct pronoun objects.

1. I know her.   4. I know him.
2. I know them.   5. I know them.
3. I know her.   6. I know her.

4 Practice the questions with noun objects and the answers with pronoun objects.

1. Do you know Mrs. Baker?   Yes, I know her.
2. Do you know Joan?   Yes, I know her.
3. Do you know Peter?   Yes, I know him.
   (*Continue.*)

5 Practice statements with the future form of the verbs for the actions shown in the pictures.

1. Mrs. Baker is going to give some shirts.   4. Tom is going to play the guitar.
2. Joan is going to make a sweater.   5. Peter is going to give a new radio.
3. Joan is going to lend money.   6. Carol is going to paint a picture.

6 Practice associating the verbs with the prepositions used for the actions shown in the pictures.

give to   make for
lend to   play for
give to   paint for

7 The teacher gives the verb. The students repeat the verb with its associated preposition.

TEACHER	STUDENTS
give	give to
make	make for
lend	lend to
play	play for
(*Continue.*)	

8 Practice the complete sentence patterns for the new verbs.

1. Mrs. Baker is going to give some shirts to Mr. Baker.
2. Joan is going to make a sweater for Mr. Baker.
3. Joan is going to lend some money to Tom.
4. Tom is going to play the guitar for the guests.
5. Peter is going to give a new radio to Mr. Baker.
6. Carol is going to paint a picture for Mr. Baker.

9 Review substituting subject pronouns for the subject nouns.

1. She is going to give some shirts to Mr. Baker.
2. She is going to make a sweater for Mr. Baker.
3. She is going to lend some money to Tom.
4. He is going to play the guitar for the guests.
5. He is going to give a new radio to Mr. Baker.
6. She is going to paint a picture for Mr. Baker.

10 Practice substituting object pronouns for the direct objects.

1. She is going to give them to Mr. Baker.
2. She is going to make it for Mr. Baker.
3. She is going to lend it to Tom.
4. He is going to play it for the guests.
5. He is going to give it to Mr. Baker.
6. She is going to paint it for Mr. Baker.

11 Practice substituting object pronouns for the indirect objects of the prepositions.

1. She is going to give them to him.
2. She is going to make it for him.
3. She is going to lend it to him.
4. He is going to play it for them.
5. He is going to give it to him.
6. She is going to paint it for him.

12 Practice questions with names and nouns and answers with subject and object pronouns.

1. Is Mrs. Baker going to give some shirts to Mr. Baker?
2. Yes, she is going to give them to him.

3. Is Joan going to make a sweater for Mr. Baker?
4. Yes, she is going to make it for him.

5. Is Joan going to lend some money to Tom?
6. Yes, she is going to lend it to him.
   (*Continue.*)

13 Summary Drill. Practice various question and answer patterns with the pictures.

1. Who is she?　She is Mrs. Baker.
2. Where does she live?　She lives in Centerville.
3. Who is he?　He is Mr. Baker.
4. What is she going to do?　She is going to give some shirts to him.
5. Why is she going to give him some shirts?　Because it is his birthday.
   (*Continue.*)

SUBSTITUTION DRILLS

1 Practice statements with object pronouns. Use the verb *know*.

Examples: Peter/him   *Peter knows him.*
           we/them   *We know them.*
           I/you   *I know you.*

1. Carol/her   7. we/him
2. Linda/him   8. you/them
3. Tom/them   9. I/her
4. Peter/us   10. she/us
5. Mr. Baker/you   11. he/them
6. Peter/me   12. Mrs. Baker/him

2 Practice questions with object pronouns. Use the verb *know*.

Examples: you/them   *Do you know them?*
           Peter/her   *Does Peter know her?*
           you/me   *Do you know me?*

1. you/him   7. you/her
2. Peter/her   8. he/me
3. Peter/them   9. she/me
4. Linda/us   10. you/us
5. they/you   11. Mr. Hill/him
6. they/me   12. Sharon/her

3 Practice negative statements with direct objects. Use the verb *like*.

Examples: he/her   *He doesn't like her.*
           she/me   *She doesn't like me.*
           I/them   *I don't like them.*

1. he/them   7. she/us
2. I/them   8. they/us
3. Tom/him   9. Mr. Baker/them
4. Tom/them   10. Jerry/him
5. I/it   11. he/him
6. she/you   12. they/us

4 Practice making requests. Use *to* or *for* before the object pronouns.

Examples: lend some money/me
               Please lend some money to me.

           play some music/them
               Please play some music for them.

           open the door/her
               Please open the door for her.

1. lend some money/him
2. give a pencil/me
3. explain the word/us
4. serve coffee/them
5. speak English/them
6. make a new dress/her
7. cook dinner/us
8. fix the car/me
9. open the door/us
10. close the window/me
11. buy some coffee/me
12. make a cake/him
13. close the door/me
14. open your book/me
15. buy a new shirt/him
16. do this drill/me

5 Practice statements with object pronouns. Use the future form of the verb.

Examples:　she/lend some money/him
She is going to lend some money to him.

Mrs. Baker/bake a cake/him
Mrs. Baker is going to bake a cake for him.

1. I/give a pencil/you
2. Mrs. Carter/make a cake/us
3. Peter/lend some money/him
4. she/buy some coffee/me
5. Linda/serve cake and ice cream/them
6. Mr. Baker/fix the car/him
7. Mrs. Carter/speak English/us
8. she/explain the long words/them
9. Carol/paint a picture/her
10. Mrs. Hill/cook breakfast/him
11. you/teach English/us
12. I/do this exercise/you
13. we/make a cake/her
14. Tom/play the guitar/them
15. Joan and Carol/sing/them
16. they/have a party/him

TRANSFORMATION DRILLS

1 Change the *italicized* words to object pronouns (me, you, him, her, it, us, them).

Examples:　Joan is going to lend some money to *Tom.*
Joan is going to lend some money to him.

Peter needs *those pencils.*
Peter needs them.

1. Carol is painting a picture for *Mr. Baker.*
2. She is cooking lunch for *Jerry and Sharon.*
3. Mr. Baker is fixing the car for *Mr. Smith.*
4. Tom is playing the guitar for *the guests.*
5. Linda likes *Tom.*
6. Tom likes *Linda,* too.
7. Mrs. Carter explains the words to *the students.*
8. She usually cooks dinner for *her husband.*
9. Joan is making *the sweater.*
10. Tom wants *those books.*
11. Linda is going to serve coffee to *the guests.*
12. Peter is going to buy a new radio for *his father.*
13. Joan is going to lend some money to *Tom.*
14. We are going to study *English.*
15. We are going to do *the next drill.*
16. We do *drills* every day.
17. I don't understand *those words.*
18. The students are writing *some sentences.*

2 Change these commands to requests by adding the word *please.*

Examples:　　**Open the door!**　(Command)
Please open the door.　(Request)

Listen to me!   (Command)
Please listen to me.   (Request)

1. Close the door!
2. Open the window!
3. Give me some milk!
4. Make a dress for her!
5. Explain this sentence to us!
6. Buy some fruit for us!
7. Go home!
8. Listen to me!
9. Write this exercise!
10. Practice these new words!
11. Study that at home tonight!
12. Go downtown and buy some new clothes!
13. Clean your room!
14. Wash the dishes for your mother!
15. Do the next drill!
16. Buy some food for the party!
17. Give this money to your brother!
18. Open the door for your friend!

3 Change the verbs in these sentences from the future to the present continuous form. Change *tomorrow* **to** *now.*

Examples: **He is going to buy a cookbook tomorrow.**
He is buying a cookbook now.

We are going to study English tomorrow.
We are studying English now.

1. Peter is going to lend some money to Tom tomorrow.
2. We are going to go downtown tomorrow.
3. He is going to cook dinner for them tomorrow.
4. He is going to fix the car for Mr. Smith tomorrow.
5. Tom is going to give a watch to his father tomorrow.
6. I am going to speak English to you tomorrow.
7. Jerry is going to study Spanish tomorrow.
8. We are going to go to the store tomorrow.
9. Carol is going to paint a picture for her tomorrow.
10. We are going to do this drill tomorrow.
11. She is going to buy a shirt for him tomorrow.
12. I am going to go to school tomorrow.

4 Change all the *italicized* **names to pronouns or possessive adjectives. Change the subject nouns to subject pronouns. Change the possessive nouns to possessive adjectives. Change the object nouns to object pronouns.**

Examples: *Peter* **is giving some money to** *Tom.*
He is giving some money to him.

Mr. Baker **is** *Joan's* **father.**
He is her father.

1. *Mrs. Baker* is cooking lunch for *Peter and Jerry.*
2. *Carol's* brother likes *Linda.*
3. *Linda* is *Jerry's* sister.
4. *Mrs. Carter* is making a dress for *Sharon.*
5. *Jerry and Peter* are talking to *Tom.*
6. *Mrs. Carter* is explaining the sentence to *Mary.*
7. *Jerry's* father is a strong man.
8. *Sharon* is *Mrs. Carter's* daughter.
9. *Mrs. Baker* has a lot of dishes.
10. *Mr. Anderson* doesn't have many neighbors.
11. *Mrs. Hill's* children are going to go to *Carol's* party.

12. *Mrs. Baker* is going to give some new shirts to *Mr. Baker.*
13. *Carol* is going to paint a picture for *Mr. Baker.*
14. *Joan and Carol* are going to sing and *Tom* is going to play the guitar.
15. *Peter* is going to ask *Tom* to open the door for *Carol.*
16. *Mr. Baker* is going to be 43 years old next Friday.
17. *The Bakers* live in Centerville.
18. *The Bakers'* house is large, but it isn't new.
19. *Mrs. Baker and the children* are going to have a party for *Mr. Baker.*
20. *Mr. Baker's* friends are going to go to his party.

WRITING PRACTICE

Choose one word for each blank space.

Next Friday is Mr. Baker's birthday. He is going to be 43 years (1)_____. Mrs. Baker and the children always give him presents on (2)_____ birthday. They are going to have a party for (3)_____ and give him presents next Friday. They are going to invite a few of his friends to the (4)_____. Mrs. Baker is going to (5)_____ a really good dinner and bake a birthday cake. Tom is (6)_____ to play the guitar for everyone, and Joan and Carol are going (7)_____ sing for them. Everyone is going to (8)_____ a wonderful time.

SITUATIONAL PRACTICE

1 Practice making requests. Ask other students to do things for you. For example:

"Please open the door for me."
"Please close the window for me."

Here are some expressions that you can use:

stand up	give me your (book)
sit down	put the (book) on the (desk)
come here	smile
open your book	walk to the (door)
close your book	

2 The student who follows the requests can say sentences. Before performing the requested action he can make a sentence with a future verb form:

"I am going to stand up."
"I am going to open the door."
(*Continue.*)

While performing the action the student can make sentences using the present continuous verb form:

"I am standing up."
"I am opening the door."
(*Continue.*)

3 Ask various students to pretend to be members of the Baker family. Discuss the party for Mr. Baker. Talk about Mr. Baker's birthday, how old he is going to be, what everyone is going to give him, what everyone is going to do at the party, and so forth.

Ask other students in the class to ask questions of the students who are pretending to be the Bakers. (You can have students hold picture cards or name tags to help them remember who they are pretending to be.)

4 Ask students to compose their own sentences using the various object pronouns. You can do this orally, on the blackboard, or on paper.

Lesson Fifteen

LISTENING DRILL

Step 1. Listen to your teacher pronounce the words below several times.
Step 2. Listen to your teacher say each word and decide if it is in column 1, 2, 3, 4, or 5.
Step 3. Answer with the number when the teacher pronounces the words.

1	2	3	4	5
boat	vote	moat	note	goat

READING

Jerry Hill is Peter Baker's friend. We talked about him before. He lives in Centerville with his father, mother, and sister. His aunt, Mrs. Carter, and Mrs. Carter's daughter, Sharon, live with the Hills. Jerry's father is a postman. He works in the Centerville post office. His aunt is a teacher, and his mother is a housewife. Jerry is a student. He attends the Centerville High School.

In this lesson we are going to talk about what Jerry did yesterday. We are going to practice the past form of verbs.

Jerry dressed before breakfast yesterday. After breakfast he walked to school. In the morning he had three classes: French, gym, and history. In his French class he practiced pronunciation and did some drills, and in his gym class he played football. In his history class the teacher talked about the American revolution. The teacher asked some questions about the revolution, and Jerry and the other students answered them.

At lunch time, Jerry talked to some of his friends, and in the afternoon he attended his geometry and art classes. Then he walked home, cleaned his room, and listened to some music before dinner.

After dinner, Jerry watched television for about two hours. Then he studied for a little while and at about ten thirty, he undressed and went to bed. It was a busy day.

"YES OR NO" QUESTIONS

Give the correct short answer.

1. Does Jerry Hill live in Centerville?
2. Is Centerville in the United States?
3. Does Jerry attend school every weekday?
4. Did he attend school yesterday?
5. Did he play football in his gym class?
6. Did he study Spanish in the afternoon?
7. Did he clean his room before dinner?
8. Did he go to a movie after dinner?
9. Did he watch television after dinner?
10. Did he undress before he went to bed?

"QUESTION WORD" QUESTIONS

Answer with complete sentences.

1. Where does Jerry Hill live?
2. Who does he live with?
3. What does he do every day?
4. What did he do before breakfast yesterday?
5. How did he go to school?
6. What did he do in his French class?
7. What did he do in his gym class?
8. Who did he talk to at lunch time?
9. How did he go home?
10. What did he do before he went to bed?

CONVERSATIONS

1   A. How did Jerry go to school yesterday?
   B. He walked because his house is near the school.
   A. What did he study at school?
   B. Oh, a lot of things: history, geometry, French, and art.
   A. What did he do after school?
   B. He walked home, cleaned his room, and listened to some music.

2   A. What did the teacher talk about in your history class yesterday?
   B. He talked about the American revolution.
   A. Did he ask you any questions about it?
   B. Yes, he asked some questions and we answered them.
   A. Did you enjoy the class?
   B. Yes, it was interesting.

3   A. Did you talk to Jerry yesterday?
   B. Yes, I talked to him at lunch time.
   A. What did you talk about?
   B. We talked about the party that Carol is going to have.
   A. Are you going to go to the party?
   B. Yes, and so is Jerry. I'm sure we are going to enjoy it.

GRAMMAR NOTES

1. WORDS FOR PAST TIME

Here are some common words which usually indicate past time:

yesterday	last January
yesterday morning	last February
yesterday afternoon	last March
yesterday evening	last year
last night	the day before yesterday
last Monday	the week before last
last Tuesday	the month before last
last Wednesday	the year before last
last week	last summer
last month	last spring

2. THE PAST FORM OF VERBS

The past form of regular verbs is written by adding "ed" to the simple verb form. (There may be some small change in the spelling of the simple form when the "ed" is added.)

The "ed" is pronounced in three different ways depending on the last sound of the simple form.

1. If the last sound of the simple form is /t/ or /d/, the "ed" is pronounced /id/:

paint	painted
need	needed
repeat	repeated
invite	invited

2. If the last sound is not /t/ or /d/ and is voiced, the "ed" is pronounced /d/:

listen	listened
play	played
answer	answered
study	studied
clean	cleaned

3. If the last sound is not /t/ or /d/ and is unvoiced, the "ed" is pronounced /t/:

dress	dressed
walk	walked
practice	practiced
talk	talked
ask	asked
watch	watched

Listen to your teacher give the simple and past forms of the regular verbs that you have studied and see if you can hear whether the past form is: 1 /id/, 2 /d/, or 3 /t/. After you are sure you can hear these differences, practice giving the past form of the verb after the teacher gives the simple form.

3. SENTENCE PATTERNS WITH PAST FORMS

Notice the following patterns of the use of the auxiliary verb, did.

A. AFFIRMATIVE STATEMENTS

In affirmative statements an auxiliary verb is not used.

Jerry dressed before breakfast yesterday.   I studied English yesterday.
He walked to school yesterday.   They needed some new books.

B. NEGATIVE STATEMENTS

In negative statements the auxiliary verb *did* is used with *not. Did* is the past form of *do.* The contraction *didn't* is often used in conversation.

I didn't work yesterday.   He didn't study Spanish yesterday.
We didn't walk to school yesterday.   She didn't go downtown last Saturday.

C. QUESTIONS

"Yes or no" questions are made with *did* before the subject.

Did Jerry dress before breakfast yesterday?   Did she serve coffee to the guests last night?
Did you practice pronunciation yesterday?   Did they watch television last Sunday?

D. TAG QUESTIONS

Tag questions follow the usual patterns with *did* as the auxiliary verb.

He dressed before breakfast, didn't he?   She talked to him last week, didn't she?
You walked downtown, didn't you?   Peter studied Spanish last night, didn't he?

4. AUXILIARY *DID* WITH THE VERB *DO*

You will remember that *do* can be both a verb and an auxiliary verb. Therefore it is common to have the verb *did* in past time expressions.

Carol did the dishes.
I did my homework last night.
Mary did that last year.

We also often have sentences with *do* as the verb and *did* as the past auxiliary.

Did you do your homework?
I didn't do it.
She didn't do her homework last night.
Why didn't she do it?

5. REGULAR & IRREGULAR VERBS

Regular verbs add "ed" to the simple form to make their past forms. English also has several irregular verbs that change in various ways to make their past forms. Here are a few examples:

go   went
eat   ate
take   took

In this lesson we practice with the past form of regular verbs. In the next lesson we will learn more about irregular verbs and practice with them.

Irregular verbs are used in past time statements and questions in the same general way as regular verbs:

Statements

He went to school yesterday.
She ate lunch.
He took a bath.

Questions

Did he go home at 6 o'clock?
Did she eat in a restaurant?
Did he take a bath?

113

dressed /t/

Before breakfast

114

walked /t/

After breakfast

115

played /d/

In his gym class

116

answered /d/

In his history class

117

talked /t/

At lunch time

118

walked /t/

After school

119

cleaned /d/

Before dinner

120

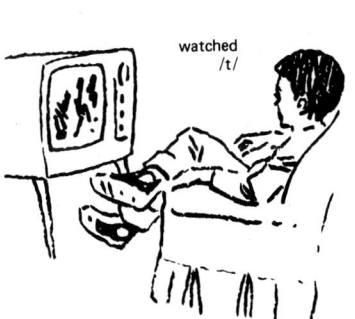

watched /t/

After dinner

PICTURE DRILLS

1 Practice the numbers from 113 to 120.

113. one hundred and thirteen   117. one hundred and seventeen
114. one hundred and fourteen   118. one hundred and eighteen
115. one hundred and fifteen   119. one hundred and nineteen
116. one hundred and sixteen   120. one hundred and twenty

2 Practice the past form verbs used in this lesson. Observe the correct pronunciation of the "ed" ending.

dressed /t/   walked /t/
played /d/   answered /d/
talked /t/   walked /t/
cleaned /d/   watched /t/

3 Practice statements with the past forms and the word *yesterday*.

1. Jerry dressed yesterday.
2. He walked to school yesterday.
3. He played football yesterday.
4. He answered some questions yesterday.

5. He talked to his friends yesterday.
6. He walked home yesterday.
7. He cleaned his room yesterday.
8. He watched television yesterday.

4 Practice the past time statements with the other time words in the pictures.

1. Jerry dressed before breakfast yesterday.
2. He walked to school after breakfast yesterday.
3. He played football in his gym class yesterday.
4. He answered some questions in his history class yesterday.

5. He talked to his friends at lunch yesterday.
6. He walked home after school yesterday.
7. He cleaned his room before dinner yesterday.
8. He watched television after dinner yesterday.

5 Practice "yes or no" questions with the past auxiliary *did*.

1. Did he dress before breakfast?
2. Did he walk to school after breakfast?
3. Did he play football in his gym class?
4. Did he answer some questions in his history class?

5. Did he talk to his friends at lunch time?
6. Did he walk home after school?
7. Did he clean his room before dinner?
8. Did he watch television after dinner?

6 Practice the questions with short answers.

1. Did he dress before breakfast yesterday?
    Yes, he did.
2. Did he walk to school before breakfast yesterday?
    No, he didn't.

3. Did he play football in his gym class yesterday?
>   Yes, he did.
4. Did he play football in his history class yesterday?
>   No, he didn't.
> (*Continue.*)

7 Practice questions with *when* and long answers.

1. When did he dress yesterday?
>   He dressed before breakfast.
2. When did he walk to school?
>   He walked to school after breakfast.
3. When did he play football?
>   He played football in his gym class.
> (*Continue.*)

8 Practice tag questions with the past forms.

1. He dressed before breakfast yesterday, didn't he?
2. He walked to school after breakfast, didn't he?
3. He played football in his gym class, didn't he?

9 Practice tag questions with short answers.

1. He dressed before breakfast yesterday, didn't he?
>   Yes, he did.
2. He walked to school before breakfast, didn't he?
>   No, he didn't.
3. He walked to school after breakfast, didn't he?
>   Yes, he did.
4. He played football in his gym class, didn't he?
>   Yes, he did.
5. He played football in his history class, didn't he?
>   No, he didn't.
> (*Continue.*)

10 Review four different verb forms.

Use the present continuous verb form with the word *now*.

Use the simple verb form with the word *every day*.

Use the "going to" future verb form with the word *tomorrow*.

Use the past verb form with the word *yesterday*.

1. now	He is dressing now.
2. every day	He dresses every day.
3. tomorrow	He is going to dress tomorrow.
4. yesterday	He dressed yesterday.

5. every day	He walks to school every day.
6. yesterday	He walked to school yesterday.
7. now	He is walking to school now.

11 Summary Drill.   Practice the various question-answer patterns that have been drilled in Lessons One to Fifteen using the pictures for this lesson.

SUBSTITUTION DRILLS

1 Review the days of the week with the word *last* indicating past time.

Examples: Monday   *last Monday*
              Tuesday   *last Tuesday*

1. Monday	5. Friday
2. Tuesday	6. Saturday
3. Wednesday	7. Sunday
4. Thursday	

2 Review the months of the year with *last* indicating past time.

Examples: January   *last January*
              February   *last February*

1. January	7. July
2. February	8. August
3. March	9. September
4. April	10. October
5. May	11. November
6. June	12. December

3 Review the seasons of the year with *last* indicating past time.

Example: spring   *last spring*

1. spring	3. fall
2. summer	4. winter

4 Practice affirmative statements with the past form of regular verbs.

Examples: he/dress/yesterday
              He dressed yesterday.

              I/walk/to school/yesterday
              I walked to school yesterday.

1. he/walk/to school/yesterday	4. Tom/study/last night
2. I/dress/before breakfast	5. he/repeat/some words/yesterday
3. I/walk/home/after school	6. you/study/last night

7. she/listen/to music/yesterday
8. Carol/cook dinner/yesterday
9. Mr. Hill/work/last week
10. Mr. Baker/fix/the car/yesterday
11. Tom and Linda/dance/last night

12. we/study/this/last Tuesday
13. she/clean/the house/last week
14. Carol/serve/coffee/last night
15. I/learn/these words/last month
16. Tom/play/his guitar/this morning

5 Practice negative statements with past time expressions.

Examples: **I/study/last night**
I didn't study last night.

Joan/work/yesterday
Joan didn't work yesterday.

1. she/work/last Monday
2. Joan/type/those letters
3. Mr. Hill/work/yesterday
4. she/cook/lunch/yesterday
5. Carol/paint/that/last year
6. Linda/talk/to Peter/yesterday
7. we/repeat/these sentences
8. I/study/this/last Sunday

9. the teacher/explain/the new words
10. they/fix/his car/last week
11. we/watch/television/last night
12. you/listen/to me/this morning
13. she/talk/to him/at lunch time
14. he/dance/with her/at the party
15. she/dance/with him/last week
16. Tom/work/on the farm/last summer

6 Practice questions with past time expressions. Use the auxiliary *did*.

Examples: **he/study/yesterday**   *Did he study yesterday?*
you/work/last week   *Did you work last week?*

1. she/work/last Friday
2. Joan/type/the letter/yesterday
3. Mrs. Hill/cook/dinner/last night
4. you/do your homework/yesterday
   afternoon
5. Mr. Hill/work/in the post office/last
   year
6. Tom/play/the guitar/at Carol's party/
   last Saturday night

7. Jerry/study/geometry and art/
   in his afternoon classes/yesterday
8. you/listen/to the teacher/in your
   history class/this morning
9. Jerry/clean his room/after school/
   yesterday
10. you/walk/downtown/after school/
    yesterday afternoon

7 Practice tag questions with past forms. Use the word *yesterday*.

Examples: **he/study**
He studied yesterday, didn't he?

she/cook/dinner
She cooked dinner yesterday, didn't she?

1. he/work
2. you/study/these words
3. they/listen/to the music
4. Jerry/walk/home
5. Jerry/study/history

6. Mrs. Baker/cook breakfast
7. Carol/paint/that picture
8. Mr. Baker/fix/the car
9. he/talk/to her
10. she/invite/him/to her party

11. Tom/dance/with Linda
12. you/listen/to me
13. you/learn/this
14. we/practice/pronunciation

8 Review four verb forms. Make affirmative statements with the words given. Use the verb form that best fits the time words given.

Use the present continuous form with the word *now.* Use the simple form with the expression *every day.* Use the "going to" future form with *tomorrow.* Use the past form with *yesterday.*

Examples:
he/work/now	*He is working now.*
he/work/every day	*He works every day.*
he/work/tomorrow	*He is going to work tomorrow.*
he/work/yesterday	*He worked yesterday.*

1. he/study/now
2. he/study/every day
3. he/study/tomorrow
4. he/study/yesterday
5. we/study/English/now
6. we/study/English/every day
7. we/study/English/tomorrow
8. we/study/English/yesterday
9. Linda/dress/now
10. Linda/dress/tomorrow
11. Linda/dress/yesterday
12. Linda/dress/every day
13. you/listen/to me/every day
14. you/listen/to me/now
15. you/listen/to me/tomorrow
16. you/listen/to me/yesterday

9 Repeat drill 8 making negative statements, then again making questions, and again making tag questions.

TRANSFORMATION DRILLS
1 Change from affirmative to negative.

Examples:
Affirmative	He studied last night.
Negative	*He didn't study last night.*

Affirmative	They walked home yesterday afternoon.
Negative	*They didn't walk home yesterday afternoon.*

1. He dressed before breakfast yesterday.
2. He walked to school yesterday morning.
3. She listened to the teacher yesterday afternoon.
4. Peter opened the window last night.
5. The students repeated the new words.
6. Mrs. Baker cooked lunch for her family yesterday.
7. I cleaned my room last week.
8. They danced at the party last Saturday night.
9. I did my homework last night.
10. She served coffee to her guests last Sunday.
11. Mrs. Carter explained that last Wednesday.
12. I watched television last night.
13. Jerry talked to Tom at lunch time yesterday.
14. We studied these sentences yesterday.
15. He is walking to school now.
16. He walks to school every day.
17. He is going to walk to school tomorrow.
18. He walked to school yesterday.

2 Change these statements to questions.

Examples: Statement **He walked to school yesterday.**
Question *Did he walk to school yesterday?*

1. They studied English yesterday.
2. Tom opened the window for Linda yesterday.
3. Mr. Baker fixed our car last week.
4. Joan typed those letters yesterday.
5. You studied history yesterday morning.
6. Peter studied Spanish in his morning class.
7. They walked home after school.
8. We wanted to buy some books.
9. We repeated these sentences yesterday.
10. Mrs. Hill cooked dinner for them last night.
11. Peter and Tom worked on their uncle's farm last summer.
12. Joan finished high school two years ago.
13. Mr. and Mrs. Baker watched television for two hours last night.
14. Mr. Hill worked in the Centerville Post Office last year.
15. We are studying English now.
16. We study English every day.
17. We are going to study English tomorrow.
18. We studied English yesterday.

3 Add tag questions to these statements.

Examples: Statement **He worked yesterday.**
Statement + tag *He worked yesterday, didn't he?*

1. He dressed before breakfast, _____?
2. Linda walked to school yesterday, _____?
3. Jerry played football in his gym class, _____?
4. Mrs. Baker cooked dinner last night, _____?
5. You learned these new words, _____?
6. We studied this last week, _____?
7. Mr. and Mrs. Hill watched television last night, _____?
8. Peter and Tom worked on their uncle's farm, _____?

4 Change the verbs from simple to past form. Change the expression *every day* to *yesterday*.

Examples: Simple **He dresses every day.**
Past *He dressed yesterday.*

1. He walks to school every day.
2. I study every day.
3. Tom plays his guitar every day.
4. Jerry talks to Carol every day.
5. Mrs. Baker cooks dinner for her family every day.
6. She dances with him every day.
7. She cleans his room every day.
8. I do my homework every day.
9. Tom plays football every day.
10. We study English in this class every day.
11. Jerry's mother and father watch television every day.
12. Mrs. Hill cooks breakfast for her family every day.

5 Change the *italicized* words to subject pronouns, possessive adjectives, or other pronouns.

Examples: *Tom* is giving a book to *Carol.*
He is giving a book to her.

Mrs. Baker cooked dinner for *Mr. Baker's* friends.
She cooked dinner for his friends.

1. *Tom* walked to school after breakfast.
2. *Carol* served coffee to *Jerry and Linda.*
3. *Peter* needed some new shoes.
4. *Mr. Baker* fixed *Mrs. Carter's* car last week.
5. *Tom* played the guitar for *Linda.*
6. *Mrs. Carter* explained the grammar to the *students* last Monday.
7. *Mr. Anderson* invited *Peter and Tom* to work on his farm.
8. *Mr. and Mrs. Anderson* don't have many neighbors.
9. *The Bakers'* house isn't new, but it is fairly large.
10. *The Bakers* are going to visit *the Andersons* next weekend.
11. *Carol* is going to buy a few cookies and a little cake.
12. *Peter* is *Tom's* brother.

WRITING PRACTICE

Choose one word for each blank space.

Jerry (1) _____ before breakfast yesterday. After breakfast he walked to (2)_____ . In the morning he had three classes: French, gym, and history. In his French (3) _____ , he practiced pronunciation and did some drills, and in his (4)_____ class, he played football. In his history (5)_____ , the teacher talked about the American revolution. The teacher asked some questions about the revolution, and Jerry and the other students answered them.

At lunch time, Jerry (6)_____ to some of his friends, and in the afternoon he attended his geometry and art classes. Then he walked home, cleaned his (7) _____ and listened to some (8) _____ before dinner.

SITUATIONAL PRACTICE

1 One student comes to the front of the room and performs an action. Then the student asks another student, "What did I do?" and the other student answers. Try to restrict actions to the regular verbs that have been practiced. If students have mastered these verbs, they may go on to additional vocabulary items. This game can be used to introduce some of the irregular verbs that are introduced in the next lesson.

2 A student goes to the front of the room, tells the class what he is going to do using the future verb form, then performs the action and tells the class what he is doing using the present continuous verb form, and finally, tells the class what he did using the past form. For example:

"I'm going to open the door."
(before performing the action)
"I'm opening the door."
(while performing the action)
"I opened the door."
(after performing the action)

The student may then ask another student what he did (as in 1).

3 Review imperatives and past forms by having two students come to the front of the room. One student asks the other to perform some action. The other student does as requested. Then the first student asks the second what he did and the second answers. For example:

First student: "Please open your book."
Second student opens book.

First student: "What did you do?"
Second student: "I opened my book."

4 Ask students past time questions such as: "What did you do yesterday?" Have students answer with as many details as possible. You may have some students give a short talk to the class telling about what they did yesterday or some other time in the past.

5 Have students compose sentences using the past form of the regular verbs that have been practiced. You may have them compose sentences on the blackboard where all the class can observe corrections, or on paper for individual correction or both.

6 Give each student a regular verb and have him compose four sentences with a different verb form in each sentence. In other words, have one sentence in the present continuous form with *now*, one sentence in the simple form with *every day*, one in the future with *tomorrow*, and one in the past with *yesterday*.

Lesson Sixteen

Linda's New Clothes

LISTENING DRILL

Step 1. Listen to your teacher pronounce the words below several times.
Step 2. Listen to your teacher say each word and decide if it is number 1, 2, 3, 4, or 5.
Step 3. Answer with the number when the teacher pronounces the words.

1	2	3	4	5
base	vase	pace	face	case

READING

We read about Linda Hill before. Linda lives in Centerville with her father, mother, brother, aunt, and cousin. Her father is a postman. He works in the Centerville post office. Her aunt is a teacher. She teaches in the Centerville High School. Linda is fourteen years old. She has black hair and brown eyes. She is a pretty girl. She is a student in junior high school now. After she finishes high school, she is going to study nursing. She is going to be a nurse.

Yesterday was Saturday so Linda didn't go to school. She went downtown and bought some new clothes. Before she went downtown, she asked her father for some money because she didn't have any. He gave her thirty dollars.

Linda rode downtown on the bus and went to a department store. She found a nice blue dress and bought it. It cost $17.95. Then she went to a restaurant and ate lunch. After lunch she went to a shoe store and bought a pair of shoes. They cost $8.95. Then she rode home on the bus and showed her new clothes to her mother. Her mother liked them very much.

Next week Linda is going to go to a party. She is going to wear her new clothes. She hopes everyone will like them.

In this lesson we are going to practice talking about what Linda did yesterday. We are going to use the past form of irregular verbs.

"YES OR NO" QUESTIONS

Give the correct short answer.

1. Did Linda go to school yesterday?
2. Did she go downtown?
3. Did she ride downtown on the bus?
4. Did she buy a red dress?
5. Did she buy a blue dress?
6. Did she eat lunch at a restaurant?
7. Did she buy a pair of shoes?
8. Is she going to go to a party next week?
9. Is she going to wear her new clothes?
10. Does she hope everyone will like her new clothes?

"OR" QUESTIONS

Answer with complete sentences.

1. Did Linda go to school or go downtown yesterday?
2. Did she buy a red dress or a blue dress?
3. Did she eat lunch in a cafeteria or a restaurant?
4. Did she ride home on a bus or a streetcar?

"QUESTION WORD" QUESTIONS

Answer with complete sentences.

1. Where does Linda Hill live?
2. Who does she live with?
3. How old is she?
4. What color are her hair and eyes?
5. Where did she go yesterday?
6. What did she buy at the department store?
7. Where did she eat lunch?
8. What did she buy at the shoe store?
9. How did she go home?
10. When is she going to go to a party?

CONVERSATIONS

1   (*Linda is talking to her father.*)

A. Dad, I want to borrow some money.
B. What do you want it for?
A. I want to buy a new dress and some shoes.
B. Do you really need them?
A. Yes, I do. I'm going to wear them to the party next week.
B. How much do you need?
A. I need about thirty dollars.
B. All right. Here is thirty dollars. Spend it carefully.

2   (*Linda is talking to a clerk in the department store.*)

A. May I help you?
B. Yes, how much is this dress?
A. It's $27.50. It's very pretty, isn't it?
B. Yes, but I don't want to spend that much.
A. This blue dress is nice. It's only $17.95.
B. Yes, I like this one. Do you have it in size 12?
A. Yes, we do. Is that going to be paid in cash or charged?
B. I'm going to pay cash.
A. Fine. Wait just a minute, please.

3   (*Linda is talking to her mother.*)

A. Mom! I'm home!
B. Hello, dear. Did you buy some clothes?

A. Yes, I did. Here's the dress.
B. Oh! It's pretty. Did you buy some shoes, too?
A. Yes, I did. Here they are.
B. These are nice, too. How much did you spend?
A. The dress cost $17.95, and the shoes cost $8.95.
B. Clothes certainly are expensive these days, aren't they?
A. Yes, they are, but these will be good for a long time.

GRAMMAR NOTES

1. PAST FORM OF IRREGULAR VERBS

English does not have a very large number of irregular verbs, but the ones it does have are used frequently. The pronunciation and spelling of the past form of each irregular verb must be learned separately.

Here are the simple and past forms of the irregular verbs that you have practiced in Lessons One through Sixteen:

SIMPLE FORM	PAST FORM
buy	bought
cost	cost
do	did
draw	drew
drive	drove
eat	ate
find	found
get	got
give	gave
go	went
have	had
know	knew
lend	lent
make	made
pay	paid
read /riyd/	read /red/
ride	rode
say	said
sing	sang
sleep	slept
speak	spoke
swim	swam
take	took
teach	taught
wear	wore
write	wrote

Practice repeating these forms after your teacher. Then see if you can give the past form after the teacher gives the simple form. If you have trouble learning these verbs, you may want to make flash cards, writing the simple form on one side and the past form on the other. See if you can give the correct past form when you look at the simple form. Then turn the card over to check your reply.

2. SENTENCE PATTERNS WITH IRREGULAR VERBS

Sentence patterns with the past form of irregular verbs are formed in exactly the same way as with regular verbs.

AFFIRMATIVE STATEMENTS

He bought a book yesterday afternoon.
Linda rode home on the bus.
Her father gave her thirty dollars.

NEGATIVE STATEMENTS

Linda didn't go to school yesterday.
He didn't have any money.
Mrs. Carter didn't teach us that yesterday.

QUESTIONS

Did she buy some new clothes yesterday?
Did Mr. Baker drive Mrs. Baker to the
    supermarket?
Did she go to a department store?

TAG QUESTIONS

He bought a new sweater, didn't he?
She ate lunch at a restaurant, didn't she?
Jerry sang a song last Sunday, didn't he?

3. NEGATIVE QUESTIONS

So far we have practiced affirmative "yes or no" questions such as:

Is this a book?   Do they go to school every day?
Are you happy?   Is she going to have a party next week?
Is he singing a song now?   Did she buy some new clothes?

All of these questions can be made negative by adding *n't* (the contraction of *not*) after the auxiliary verb.

Isn't this a book?   Don't they go to school every day?
Aren't you happy?   Isn't she going to have a party next week?
Isn't he singing a song now?   Didn't she buy some new clothes?

Negative question patterns are frequently used by English speakers. It is important to note that the answer to a question remains the same whether the affirmative or negative form of the question is used. For example with reference to the reading material for this lesson:

Is Linda fourteen years old?   Yes, she is.
Isn't Linda fourteen years old?   Yes, she is.

Does she live in New York?   No, she doesn't.
Doesn't she live in New York?   No, she doesn't.

Did she go to school yesterday?   No, she didn't.
Didn't she go to school yesterday?   No, she didn't.

The answer refers to the facts of the situation rather than being affected by whether the question is affirmative or negative. Here is one more example:

(Peter is a boy.)
Is Peter a boy? Yes, he is.
Isn't Peter a boy? Yes, he is.

121

122

123

124

125

126

127

128

129

130

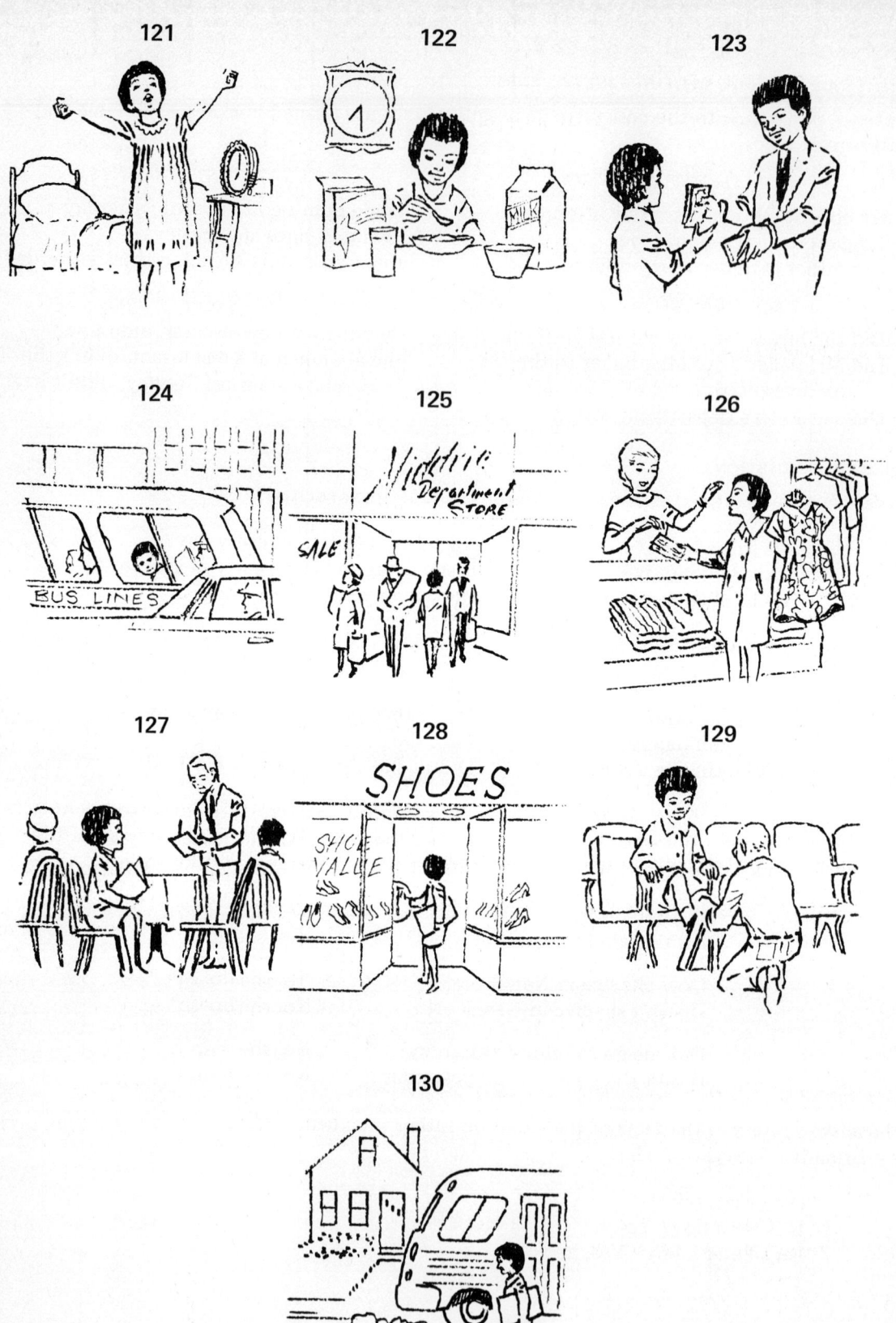

PICTURE DRILLS

1 Practice the numbers from 121 to 130.

121. One hundred and twenty-one
122. One hundred and twenty-two
123. One hundred and twenty-three
124. One hundred and twenty-four
125. One hundred and twenty-five

126. One hundred and twenty-six
127. One hundred and twenty-seven
128. One hundred and twenty-eight
129. One hundred and twenty-nine
130. One hundred and thirty

2 Practice the past forms of the irregular verbs in the pictures.

121. got up	122. ate
123. gave	124. rode
125. went	126. bought
127. ate	128. went
129. bought	130. rode

3 Practice past forms.

The teacher gives the simple form of the verbs in the pictures. The students give the past forms.

TEACHER	STUDENTS
get up	got up
eat	ate
give	gave
(Continue.)	

4 Practice affirmative statements with the past form of the irregular verbs.

1. Linda got up at eight o'clock yesterday.
2. She ate breakfast at eight-thirty yesterday.
3. Her father gave her thirty dollars yesterday.
4. She rode downtown on the bus yesterday.
5. She went to a department store yesterday.

6. She bought a blue dress yesterday.
7. She ate lunch at a restaurant yesterday.
8. She went to a shoe store yesterday.
9. She bought a pair of shoes yesterday.
10. She rode home on the bus yesterday.

5 Practice past time questions with affirmative answers.

1. Did Linda get up at eight o'clock yesterday?
    Yes, she did.
2. Did she eat breakfast at eight-thirty?
    Yes, she did.
3. Did her father give her thirty dollars?
    Yes, he did.
4. Did she ride downtown on the bus?
    Yes, she did.
5. Did she go to a department store?
    Yes, she did.
    (Continue.)

6 Practice negative questions with short answers.

1. Didn't she get up at eight o'clock yesterday?
    Yes, she did.
2. Didn't she eat breakfast at eight-thirty?
    Yes, she did.
3. Didn't her father give her thirty dollars?
    Yes, he did.
4. Didn't she ride downtown on the bus?
    Yes, she did.
    (*Continue.*)

7 Practice affirmative or negative questions with long answers.

1. Didn't she get up at seven o'clock yesterday?
    No, she didn't. She got up at eight o'clock.
2. Did she get up at seven o'clock yesterday?
    No, she didn't. She got up at eight o'clock.
3. Did she eat breakfast at seven-thirty?
    No, she didn't. She ate breakfast at eight-thirty.
4. Didn't she ride downtown on the streetcar?
    No, she didn't. She rode downtown on the bus.
5. Did she go to a book store?
    No, she didn't. She went to a department store.
    (*Continue.*)

8 Practice past time statements with tag questions.

1. She got up at eight o'clock, didn't she?
2. She ate breakfast at eight-thirty, didn't she?
3. Her father gave her thirty dollars, didn't he?
4. She rode downtown on the bus, didn't she?
    (*Continue.*)

9 Review and practice statements with four verb forms. Use the verb form that best fits the time word given.

now	She is getting up now.
every day	She gets up every day.
tomorrow	She is going to get up tomorrow.
yesterday	She got up yesterday.
now	She is eating breakfast now.
tomorrow	She is going to eat breakfast tomorrow.
every day	She eats breakfast every day.
yesterday	She ate breakfast yesterday.
(*Continue.*)	

(Be careful not to use "every day" in situations where it would be inappropriate such as: "She buys a blue dress every day.")

10 Practice negative questions with the four verb forms.

now	Isn't she getting up now?
every day	Doesn't she get up every day?
tomorrow	Isn't she going to get up tomorrow?
yesterday	Didn't she get up yesterday?
(*Continue.*)	

11 Summary Drill. Practice various question-answer patterns with the pictures for this lesson.

SUBSTITUTION DRILLS

1 Practice statements with the past form of irregular verbs.

Examples: she/eat/lunch   *She ate lunch yesterday.*
I/write/a letter   *I wrote a letter yesterday.*

1. he/buy/a jacket
2. I/do/my work
3. she/draw/a picture
4. Mr. Baker/drive/the car
5. we/eat/lunch/at home
6. she/find/some money
7. she/get up/at eight o'clock
8. he/give/her a book
9. they/go/downtown
10. she/have/a party
11. I/know/that
12. Peter/lend/him some money
13. she/make/a cake
14. we/read/this lesson
15. they/sing/a song
16. I/speak/English
17. we/swim
18. he/take/a bath
19. Mrs. Carter/teach
20. Linda/wear/her new blue dress

2 Review affirmative statements with the past form of regular verbs.

Examples: he/attend/school   *He attended school yesterday.*
they/dance   *They danced yesterday.*

1. she/cook/dinner
2. the teacher/answer/my question
3. Mrs. Baker/clean/the house
4. Tom/listen/to music
5. I/finish/that
6. Jerry/walk/home
7. he/play/football
8. everyone/work
9. he/dress/before breakfast
10. Peter/talk/to Jerry
11. Jerry/ask/a question
12. she/invite/a lot of guests
13. we/learn/this
14. we/need/some books
15. Mr. Baker/fix/our car
16. they/watch/television
17. I/study/history
18. the Bakers/visit/the Andersons
19. I/remember/his name
20. Carol/paint/a picture

3 Compare the past forms of regular and irregular verbs in affirmative statements. Use the time words given.

Examples: he/work/last week   *He worked last week.*
Jerry/sing/last Sunday   *Jerry sang last Sunday.*

1. her husband/die/last year
2. Linda/ride/downtown on the bus/yesterday
3. they/swim/in the pool/last Saturday afternoon
4. we/practice/these sentences/yesterday
5. she/find/some money/the day before yesterday
6. Joan/type/those letters/last night
7. he/give/her a new watch/last week
8. Mr. Baker/carry/the heavy things
9. Peter/know/all the answers/yesterday
10. Jerry/undress/before he went to bed
11. I/write/those sentences/last night
12. he/want/to buy a new shirt
13. she/wear/her new clothes/to the party/last Sunday
14. I/take/a bath/yesterday
15. he/sleep/at his friend's house/last night
16. Mrs. Carter/teach/English/last year

4 Practice affirmative questions in past time.

Examples: he/speak/English
              Did he speak English?

              you/go/downtown/yesterday
              Did you go downtown yesterday?

1. he/write/a letter/last night
2. she/wear/her new shoes/to the party/ last week
3. you/teach/English/last year
4. Jerry/take/a bath/last night
5. he/read/that book/last week
6. her father/lend/her/some money/ yesterday
7. they/go/home/before dinner/yesterday
8. we/do/these sentences/yesterday
9. Mrs. Baker/buy/some food/last Saturday
10. you/practice/those new words/last night

5 Practice negative questions in past time.

Examples: he/speak/English
              Didn't he speak English?

              you/go/downtown/yesterday
              Didn't you go downtown yesterday?

1. he/get up/at seven-thirty/yesterday morning
2. Peter/go/to school/yesterday
3. Mr. Baker/fix/their car/last week
4. you/learn/this/yesterday
5. Linda/dance/with Tom/at the party
6. we/do/this drill/last Monday
7. they/go/to New York/last summer
8. he/lend/you/some money/last week
9. you/eat/lunch/at school/today
10. Mr. and Mrs. Hill/watch/television/last night

6 Practice negative questions with four different verb forms. Use the verb form that best fits the time word given.

Examples: they/swim/now   *Aren't they swimming now?*
              they/swim/every day   *Don't they swim every day?*
              they/swim/tomorrow   *Aren't they going to swim tomorrow?*
              they/swim/yesterday   *Didn't they swim yesterday?*

1. he/speak English now
2. he/speak English/every day
3. he/speak English/tomorrow
4. he/speak English/yesterday

5. we/practice/now
6. we/practice/every day
7. we/practice/tomorrow
8. we/practice/yesterday
9. Carol/read/now
10. Carol/read/every day
11. Carol/read/tomorrow
12. Carol/read/yesterday
13. Tom/dress/now
14. Tom/dress/tomorrow
15. Tom/dress/yesterday
16. Tom/dress/every day
17. they/listen/every day
18. they/listen/tomorrow
19. they/listen/yesterday
20. they/listen/now
21. Mr. Hill/work/now
22. Mr. Hill/work/yesterday
23. Mr. Hill/work/every day
24. Mr. Hill/work/tomorrow

TRANSFORMATION DRILLS

1 Change the verbs in these statements from simple to past form.

Examples: Simple He speaks English in class.
           Past   *He spoke English in class.*

           Simple He has a good radio.
           Past   *He had a good radio.*

1. She sings.
2. I read the lessons.
3. Peter knows the answer to the question.
4. Linda rides to school on the bus.
5. Jerry needs a good red shirt.
6. Peter and Tom go to high school.
7. He gives her money.
8. I get up at six-thirty in the morning.
9. Mrs. Baker cooks dinner for her family.
10. Mr. Hill eats breakfast at seven-fifteen in the morning.
11. Mr. Baker drives Mrs. Baker to the supermarket.
12. Carol draws pictures.
13. I do my homework.
14. Jerry sings in church.
15. Mrs. Baker buys food at the supermarket.
16. Mrs. Carter makes clothes for Sharon.
17. He sleeps for eight hours.
18. Jerry takes a bath before he goes to bed.
19. The Bakers visit the Andersons on the weekend.
20. I undress before I go to bed.

2 Change these statements from affirmative to negative.

Examples: Affirmative He spoke English.
           Negative   *He didn't speak English.*

           Affirmative She is working now.
           Negative   *She isn't working now.*

1. He taught them some new words.
2. She wore her new dress.
3. Jerry is doing his homework now.
4. I went home after school yesterday.
5. Mrs. Carter explained that yesterday.
6. He wants to go to school.
7. She wanted some coffee.
8. Linda is going to need some money.
9. Her brother had some money last week.
10. They spoke Spanish.
11. Carol and Joan are going to sing a song for us.
12. I read that book last year.
13. Mrs. Hill made some cookies for them.
14. I knew the answer to question number eight.
15. They ate lunch at school yesterday.
16. She loved him very much.

3 Change these questions from affirmative to negative.

Examples:	Affirmative	Did she go downtown yesterday?
	Negative	*Didn't she go downtown yesterday?*
	Affirmative	Does she have school on Saturday?
	Negative	*Doesn't she have school on Saturday?*

1. Did she want to buy a new dress?
2. Is she fourteen years old?
3. Did Linda go downtown yesterday?
4. Did she ride downtown on the bus?
5. Is she going to go to a party next week?
6. Do Peter and Jerry attend high school?
7. Does Linda hope that everyone will like her new clothes?
8. Is this number eight?
9. Did you have a good time last night?
10. Are Mr. and Mrs. Baker going to watch television tonight?
11. Is Linda going to dance with Tom Baker?
12. Do you like coffee?
13. Does he want to buy some new clothes?
14. Is this drill difficult?
15. Did you read any good books last year?
16. Is English an easy language to learn?

4 Add tag questions to these statements.

Examples:	Statement	Linda went downtown.
	Statement + tag	*Linda went downtown, didn't she?*
	Statement	English is an easy language.
	Statement + tag	*English is an easy language, isn't it?*

1. We read about Linda Hill before, _____ ?
2. She lives in Centerville, _____ ?
3. Her father is a postman, _____ ?
4. Her aunt is a teacher, _____ ?
5. She teaches in the Centerville High School, _____ ?
6. Linda is fourteen years old, _____ ?
7. She is student in junior high school, _____ ?
8. She is going to study nursing, _____ ?
9. She is going to be a nurse, _____ ?
10. Her father gave her thirty dollars, _____ ?
11. Linda rode downtown on the bus, _____ ?
12. She bought a blue dress in a department store, _____ ?
13. She ate lunch at a restaurant, _____ ?
14. She showed her new clothes to her mother, _____ ?
15. She is going to go to a party, _____ ?
16. She is going to wear her new clothes, _____ ?

WRITING PRACTICE

Choose one word for each blank space.

Linda rode downtown on the (1) _____ and went to a department store. She found a nice blue (2) _____ and bought it. It cost $17.95. Then she (3) _____ to a restaurant and ate lunch. After lunch, she went to a shoe store and (4) _____ a pair of shoes. They cost $8.95. Then she rode (5) _____ on the bus and showed her new clothes to (6) _____ mother. Her mother liked them very much.

Next week, Linda is (7) _____ to go to a party. She is going to wear her (8) _____ clothes. She hopes everyone will like them.

SITUATIONAL PRACTICE

1 Give a short talk to the class about what you did yesterday.

2 One student performs an action and then asks another student:

"What did I do?"

The second student then answers the question.

3 Ask several students to come to the front of the room. Find out what each student did after school yesterday (or some other specific time in the past). Then ask other students questions about what the students in the front of the room did.

4 Practice three verb forms by going to the front of the room and:

1. Tell the class what action you are going to perform.
2. Perform the action and tell the class what you are doing.
3. Finish the action and tell the class what you did.

For example:

1. (Before the action)   "I am going to open the window."
2. (During the action)   "I am opening the window."
3. (After the action)   "I opened the window."

5 A variation of the game in 4 can be done as follows:

Student A: "I'm going to open the window."
            "What am I going to do?"
Student B: "You're going to open the window."
Student A: (While opening the window) "What am I doing?"
Student B: "You're opening the window."
Student A: (After opening the window) "What did I do?"
Student B: "You opened the window."

6 The teacher may wish to introduce some new verbs if the students have mastered the ones practiced in Lessons One through Sixteen.

Lesson Seventeen

Nobody Was Home Last Night

LISTENING DRILL

Step 1. Listen to your teacher pronounce the words below several times.
Step 2. Listen to your teacher say each word and decide if it is number 1, 2, 3, 4, or 5.
Step 3. Answer with the number when the teacher pronounces the words.

1	2	3	4	5
fail	pale	rail	wail	whale

READING

Jerry Hill went over to the Bakers' house last night. He wanted to talk to Peter Baker. He rang the bell at the Bakers' house, but nobody answered it. Nobody was home, so he went back to his house, watched television for a while, and then went to bed.

This morning he called up Peter on the telephone. He asked where everyone was last night. Peter said that his mother and father were at a friend's house. They were playing cards. His sister, Carol, was at the library. She was studying history. His brother, Tom, was at the school gym. He was playing basketball. Peter and his sister, Joan, were at a theater. They were seeing a movie.

Peter said he was sorry that he wasn't home last night. He invited Jerry to come over to his house again tonight. Jerry is going to go over to Peter's house about eight o'clock. Peter and Jerry are going to talk and listen to some new records that Peter bought last week.

"YES OR NO" QUESTIONS

Give the correct short answer.

1. Did Jerry go over to Peter's house last night?
2. Was Peter at home?
3. Weren't Mr. and Mrs. Baker at home last night?
4. Were they at a friend's house?
5. Wasn't Tom at home either?
6. Was he at the school gym?
7. Were Peter and Joan at home?
8. Were they at a theater?
9. Is Jerry going to go over to Peter's house again tonight?
10. Are Peter and Jerry going to listen to some new records?

"TAG" QUESTIONS

Give the correct short answer.

1. Jerry went over to the Bakers' house last night, didn't he?
2. Peter wasn't home, was he?
3. Mr. and Mrs. Baker weren't home, either, were they?
4. Jerry is going to go over to the Bakers' house again tonight, isn't he?

"QUESTION WORD" QUESTIONS

Answer with complete sentences.

1. Where did Jerry go last night?
2. Who was at home at the Bakers' house last night?
3. Where were Mr. and Mrs. Baker?
4. What were they doing?
5. Where was Carol?
6. What was she doing?
7. Where was Tom?
8. What was he doing?
9. When is Jerry going to go over to the Bakers' house again?
10. What are Peter and Jerry going to do?

CONVERSATIONS

(*Peter and Jerry are talking on the telephone.*)

1 A. Hello, Peter?
   B. Yes, this is Peter. Who is this?
   A. This is Jerry. How are you?
   B. I'm fine. How are you?
   A. Fine. Where were you last night?
   B. I was at a theater with Joan. Did you call?
   A. No, I went over to your house, but nobody was home.
   B. I'm sorry. We were all out last night.

2 A. Where were your mother and father last night?
   B. They were at a friend's house.
   A. What were they doing?
   B. They were playing cards.
   A. Was Carol there, too?
   B. No, she was at the library. She was studying history.

3 A. Are you going to be home tonight?
   B. Yes, I am. Do you want to come over?
   A. Yes, I want to talk to you.
   B. Good, and I bought some new records that I want you to hear.
   A. Fine. What time shall I come over?
   B. Is about eight o'clock all right with you?
   A. That's fine. I'll see you about eight.

GRAMMAR NOTES

1. MORE ADJECTIVES

In Lessons Six, Seven, and Eight you learned several adjectives. In this lesson you will review those adjectives and practice these new ones:

hungry   tired
thirsty   busy

2. PAST FORMS OF BE

The verb *be* is often called a linking verb because it connects two parts of a sentence. Its forms and functions are quite different from other verbs in English.

We have practiced with *be* and three of its forms: *am*, *is*, and *are*. In this lesson we are going to practice with the past forms of *be*. These are *was* and *were*. Here are the patterns:

PRESENT	PAST
I am	I was
you are	you were
he is	he was
she is	she was
it is	it was
we are	we were
you are	you were
they are	they were

Sentence patterns with *was* and *were* as linking verbs are similar to the patterns with *am*, *is*, and *are*:

STATEMENTS

I am here.	I was here.
You are happy.	You were happy.
He is sick.	He was sick.

QUESTIONS

Am I here?	Was I here?
Are you happy?	Were you happy?
Is he sick?	Was he sick?

NEGATIVE STATEMENTS

I am not busy.	I was not busy.
You are not tired.	You were not tired.
She is not happy.	She was not happy.

(The contractions *wasn't* and *weren't* are frequently used.)

NEGATIVE QUESTIONS

Aren't you busy?	Weren't you busy?
Isn't he tired?	Wasn't he tired?
Aren't they happy?	Weren't they happy?

3. PAST CONTINUOUS VERB FORM

We have practiced the present continuous verb form which is made with *am*, *is*, or *are* as the auxiliary and the *-ing* ending on the main verb:

He is singing.
You are listening to music.
I am reading a book.

The past continuous verb form is made in a similar way using *was* or *were* as the auxiliaries:

STATEMENTS	QUESTIONS
I was working last week.	Were you working last week?
You were studying yesterday.	Was he playing basketball?
He was playing basketball.	Were they seeing a movie?
She was studying history.	

NEGATIVE STATEMENTS	*NEGATIVE QUESTIONS*

NEGATIVE STATEMENTS	*NEGATIVE QUESTIONS*
I was not listening to you.	Weren't you listening to me?
We were not playing football.	Wasn't he singing a song?
He was not writing a letter.	Wasn't she cooking dinner?

(The contractions *wasn't* and *weren't* are often used.)

The past continuous verb form is not as common as the ordinary past form in English. In most situations the ordinary past form is used. The past continuous form is often used to emphasize the idea that one action in the past was happening while another action happened.

4. NEGATIVE STATEMENTS WITH "TAG" QUESTIONS

Tag questions may be added to both affirmative and negative statements.

If the statement is affirmative, the tag question is negative.

He is here, isn't he?
They are studying, aren't they?
He has a farm, doesn't he?
She is going to have a party, isn't she?
Tom got up at eight o'clock, didn't he?

If the statement is negative, the tag question is affirmative.

He isn't here, is he?
They aren't studying, are they?
He doesn't have a farm, does he?
She isn't going to have a farm, is she?
Tom didn't get up at eight o'clock, did he?

5. PRONUNCIATION OF "TAG" QUESTIONS

The tag ending may be pronounced with two different intonations. If a rising intonation is used, the speaker emphasizes that he is asking a question. If a falling intonation is used, the speaker does not emphasize the question and merely indicates that the listener is invited to agree or disagree with the statement.

131

Mr. and Mrs. Baker

At a friend's house

132

Carol

At the library

133

Tom

At the school gym

134

Peter and Joan

At the theater

PICTURE DRILLS

1 Practice the numbers from 131 to 134.

131. One hundred and thirty-one
132. One hundred and thirty-two
133. One hundred and thirty-three
134. One hundred and thirty-four

2 Practice the locations with the preposition *at*.

1. at a friend's house
2. at the library
3. at the school gym
4. at a theater

3 Practice past time statements with *was* and *were*.

1. Mr. and Mrs. Baker were at a friend's house.
2. Carol was at the library.
3. Tom was at the school gym.
4. Peter and Joan were at a theater.

4 Practice questions with *where* and answers.

1. Where were Mr. and Mrs. Baker last night?
      They were at a friend's house.
2. Where was Carol last night?
      She was at the library.
   (*Continue.*)

5 Practice statements with past continuous verb forms.

1. Mr. and Mrs. Baker were playing cards last night.
2. Carol was studying history last night.
3. Tom was playing basketball last night.
4. Peter and Joan were seeing a movie last night.

6 Practice questions and answers with past continuous verb forms.

1. What were Mr. and Mrs. Baker doing last night?
      They were playing cards.
2. What was Carol doing last night?
      She was studying history.
   (*Continue.*)

7 Practice a pattern of related statements.

1. Mr. and Mrs. Baker were at a friend's house last night.
   They were playing cards.

2. Carol was at the library last night.
   She was studying history.

3. Tom was at the school gym last night.
   He was playing basketball.

4. Peter and Joan were at a theater last night.
   They were seeing a movie.

8 Practice a pattern of related questions and answers.

1. Where were Mr. and Mrs. Baker last night?
     They were at a friend's house.
2. What were they doing?
     They were playing cards.
3. Where was Carol last night?
     She was at the library.
4. What was she doing?
     She was studying history.
   (*Continue.*)

9 Practice "yes or no" questions with *was* and *were* and short answers.

1. Were Mr. and Mrs. Baker at home last night?   No, they weren't.
2. Were they at a friend's house?   Yes, they were.
3. Were they playing cards?   Yes, they were.
4. Was Carol at home last night?   No, she wasn't.
5. Was she at a friend's house?   No, she wasn't.
6. Was she at the library?   Yes, she was.
7. Was she playing cards?   No, she wasn't.
8. Was she studying history?   Yes, she was.
   (*Continue.*)

10 Practice affirmative statements with tag questions and short answers.

1. Mr. and Mrs. Baker were at home last night, weren't they?
     No, they weren't.
2. They were at a friend's house, weren't they?
     Yes, they were.
3. They were playing cards, weren't they?
     Yes, they were.
4. Carol was at home last night, wasn't she?
     No, she wasn't.
   (*Continue.*)

11 Practice negative statements with tag questions and short answers.

1. Mr. and Mrs. Baker weren't home last night, were they?
       No, they weren't.
2. They weren't at a friend's house, were they?
       Yes, they were.
3. They weren't playing cards, were they?
       Yes, they were.
    (*Continue.*)

12 Practice mixing affirmative and negative statements with tag questions. Ask other students to give short answers. Notice that the answer refers to the situation and does not change whether the question is affirmative or negative.

13 Summary Drill.   Use the pictures for this lesson to practice various question-and-answer patterns.

SUBSTITUTION DRILLS

1 Practice statements with *was* and *were* as linking verbs.

Examples:	I/hungry	*I was hungry.*
	they/difficult lessons	*They were difficult lessons.*

1. I/sad
2. they/easy books
3. you/a good student
4. he/thirty years old
5. he/tired
6. they/rich women
7. they/rich people
8. he/strong boy
9. they/bad boys
10. he/very old
11. it/blue dress
12. we/happy students

2 Practice affirmative questions with *was* and *were* as linking verbs.

Examples:	you/happy	*Were you happy?*
	he/an old man	*Was he an old man?*

1. you/tired
2. he/busy
3. they/busy
4. she/pretty
5. they/pretty
6. you/tired
7. Jerry/busy
8. Mr. Baker/at home
9. he/a handsome man
10. they/handsome men
11. she/a little girl
12. they/little girls
13. we/good students
14. I/a good student
15. Peter and Jerry/busy
16. Mr. and Mrs. Baker/at home

3 Practice negative questions with *was* and *were* as linking verbs.

Examples: you/happy *Weren't you happy?*
          he/an old man *Wasn't he an old man?*

1. he/poor	9. Tom/a young boy
2. they/rich	10. Sharon/a little girl
3. he/tired	11. we/intelligent
4. they/thirsty	12. you/hungry
5. she/a beautiful girl	13. they/beautiful girls
6. he/big	14. he/a big man
7. he/intelligent	15. you/tired
8. you/busy	16. Carol/tired

4 Practice statements with *was* and *were* and tag questions.

Examples: he/tired *He was tired, wasn't he?*
          you/busy *You were busy, weren't you?*

1. the lesson/difficult	9. that lesson/easy
2. she/pretty	10. Mrs. Hill/in the kitchen
3. Peter/at a theater	11. she/busy
4. Peter/busy	12. I/a good student
5. you/tired	13. they/new books
6. they/good students	14. Linda/downtown
7. he/an old man	15. she/in her bedroom
8. they/young men	16. this drill/easy

5 Practice statements with past continuous verb forms.

Examples: he/swim/yesterday *He was swimming yesterday.*
          we/dance/last night *We were dancing last night.*

1. Tom/play/basketball/last night	9. she/work/in an office/last winter
2. Carol/study/history/last night	10. we/see/a movie/last night
3. they/dance/at the party/last week	11. Mr. and Mrs. Baker/play/cards/last night
4. Mr. Baker/live/in Centerville/last year	12. we/study/English/yesterday
5. Mr. Hill/work/in the post office/last year	13. Jerry/listen/to music/yesterday afternoon
6. I/study/mathematics/last night	14. we/write/sentences/when the bell rang
7. Linda/make/a dress/last Sunday	15. she/cook/dinner/when you called
8. we/visit/our uncle/last summer	

6 Repeat exercise 5 above making *negative* statements.

7 Practice questions with the past continuous verb form.

Examples: he/work yesterday *Was he working yesterday?*
          you/study/last night *Were you studying last night?*

1. Jerry/study/law/yesterday   2. they/live/in the country/last year

3. Peter/study/engineering/last year
4. they/dance/last night
5. she/take/a bath/at nine-thirty/last night
6. she/make/a cake/yesterday afternoon
7. Mrs. Hill/clean/the house/yesterday afternoon
8. Peter and Jerry/listen/to music/last night
9. they/study/art/last fall
10. Mr. and Mrs. Hill/watch/television/last night
11. you/do/your homework/when I called
12. they/listen/to the teacher/in class this morning
13. Mr. Hill/work/in the post office/last year
14. Tom/play/basketball/last night
15. you/listen/to me/when I sang that song

8 Repeat exercise 7 above making negative questions.

9 Repeat exercise 7 above making affirmative statements with tag questions.

10 Repeat exercise 7 above making negative statements with tag questions.

TRANSFORMATION DRILLS

1 Change the linking verbs from present to past form. Change *am*, *is*, and *are* to *was* or *were*.

Examples:

Present	I am happy.
Past	*I was happy.*

Present	You are tired.
Past	*You were tired.*

Present	He is hungry.
Past	*He was hungry.*

1. I am sad.
2. They are busy.
3. Carol is hungry.
4. He is an intelligent boy.
5. She is here.
6. She is at a theater.
7. Mr. Baker is in the office.
8. Mrs. Baker is in the kitchen.
9. Tom is in the school gym.
10. Peter and Jerry are in Peter's room.
11. He is a rich man.
12. That is a difficult lesson.
13. I am a good student.
14. Those books are difficult to read.
15. Mr. Hill is in the dining room.

2 Change the verbs from the present continuous to the past continuous.

Examples:

Present continuous	I am studying English.
Past continuous	*I was studying English.*

Present continuous	They are playing football.
Past continuous	*They were playing football.*

1. I am working.
2. We are speaking English.
3. Carol and Linda are singing an old song.
4. The students are reading their books.
5. Peter is lending some money to Tom.
6. She is going downtown on the bus.

7. He is giving her a present.
8. The Bakers are eating dinner in the dining room.
9. Peter is driving his father's car.
10. She is drawing a pretty picture.
11. They are doing it.
12. She is buying some food for dinner.

13. The teacher is teaching grammar.
14. She is wearing a blue dress, yellow shoes, and a yellow hat.
15. Tom is playing basketball in the school gym.
16. Mr. and Mrs. Baker are playing cards at a friend's house.

3 Change these statements to questions. Notice that there are five different verb forms in these sentences.

Examples: Statement **You are working now.**
Question *Are you working now?*

Present Continuous
1. He is studying now.
2. She is typing a letter now.
3. They are working in the garage now.

Simple
4. He gets up at seven o'clock every morning.
5. She has a new green dress.
6. Peter and Jerry go to high school every day.

Future
7. Carol is going to have a party.
8. They are going to go to the supermarket.
9. I am going to see you tomorrow.

Past
10. Tom studied music yesterday.
11. Linda went to a department store.
12. They played basketball last night.

Past Continuous
13. They were dancing last night.
14. Tom was playing basketball.
15. We were speaking English.

4 Add tag questions to these statements.

(*Add negative tags to affirmative statements. Add affirmative tags to negative statements.*)

Examples: **He is working now,** *isn't he?* **He isn't dancing now,** *is he?*
She went downtown, *didn't she?* **She didn't go to school,** *did she?*
You were tired, *weren't you?* **You weren't sick,** *were you?*

1. He is here, _____?
2. They are hungry, _____?
3. She is cooking dinner, _____?
4. You like coffee, _____?
5. We are going to go to a movie, _____?
6. They drove downtown, _____?
7. They were listening to music, _____?
8. They aren't here, _____?
9. You aren't tired, _____?
10. She isn't wearing her yellow dress, _____?

WRITING PRACTICE

Choose one word for each blank space.

Jerry Hill went over to the Baker's house last (1) _____ . He rang the bell, but nobody answered it. Nobody was home.

This morning he called up Peter on the (2) _____ . He asked where everyone was last night. Peter said that his mother and father (3) _____ at a friend's house. They were playing cards. His (4)_____ , Carol, was at the library. She was studying history. His brother, Tom, was at the school gym. He was (5) _____ basketball. Peter and his sister, Joan, were at a theater. They (6) _____ seeing a movie.

Peter said he was sorry that he (7) _____ home last night. He asked Jerry to come over again (8)_____ .

SITUATIONAL PRACTICE

1 Make five flash cards with the names of verb forms on them. Use a separate card for each verb form as follows:

SIMPLE	PRESENT CONTINUOUS	FUTURE
PAST		PAST CONTINUOUS

You can use these cards in many different ways to review the five verb forms in the various sentence patterns that have been introduced. For example:

A. Write a verb on the blackboard. Show the cards with verb forms to the students and ask them to make sentences using the verb forms on the cards.

B. Ask five students to come to the front of the room. Give each one a verb-form card. Then say a verb and ask each student to say a sentence using the verb-form on his card. You can exchange the cards so each student has a chance to practice with all the verb-forms.

C. Give students a verb-form card and ask them to write a sentence on the blackboard using the verb-form on their card.

D. Say a sentence and ask students to tell the name of the verb-form that you used.

You may be able to think of other ways to use the verb cards that are particularly suitable to your classroom situation.

2 Ask students to pretend to be members of the Baker family. Ask other students to ask each member of the family where they were last night, and what they were doing. You can also ask other questions such as how old they are, what color their hair and eyes are, and what other members of their family were doing last night. (*Continue.*)

3 Ask students to give short talks to the class telling their name, where they live, what they do every day, how old they are, what they like, and what they don't like. (*Continue.*)

After a student finishes his talk, ask other students questions about the person who just spoke. You can also ask the students to ask the speaker questions.

Review

LESSON 1

OPTIONAL

Review the conversations, reading, and picture drills for this lesson.

MULTIPLE-CHOICE

Choose the best sentence of the three in each group. Mark your answer in the book or on a separate answer sheet following your teacher's instructions.

1. A) This is a book.
   B) This a book is.
   C) This a is book.

2. A) That is a house.
   B) That a house is.
   C) That a is house.

3. Is this a desk?
   A) Yes, desk.
   B) Yes, is desk.
   C) Yes, it is.

4. Is that a bank?
   A) No, that not.
   B) No, is not.
   C) No, it isn't.

5. A) Is this a hat?
   B) Is a hat this?
   C) Is hat this?

6. A) Is that house?
   B) Is that a house?
   C) Is house that?

WRITING EXERCISE

Write the answers to the following questions on a separate sheet of paper. Write complete sentences. Have the teacher correct the answers. Then put the corrected answers into a paragraph.

1. What town is in the United States?
2. Is it a large town?
3. What is a large building in Centerville?
4. What is a small building?

LESSON 2

OPTIONAL

Review the conversations, reading, and picture drills for this lesson.

MULTIPLE-CHOICE

Choose the best sentence of the three in each group. Mark your answer according to your teacher's instructions.

1. A) This is books.
   B) These are books.
   C) These is books.

2. Are these stores?
   A) Yes, are stores.
   B) Yes, they stores.
   C) Yes, they are.

3. Are those pencils?
   A) No, they not.
   B) No, they aren't.
   C) No, are not.

4. A) This are shirts.
   B) That are shirts.
   C) Those are shirts.

5. A) This is house.
   B) This is a houses.
   C) This is a house.

6. Is that a house?
   A) Yes, that house.
   B) Yes, is house.
   C) Yes, it is.

WRITING EXERCISE

Write the answers to the following questions on a separate sheet of paper. Write complete sentences. Have the teacher correct the answers. Then put the corrected answers into a paragraph.

1. Is one of the buildings in Centerville the Bakers' house?
2. Are there eight rooms in the Bakers' house?
3. Are there three people in the Baker family?
4. Who are the people in the Baker family?

LESSON 3

OPTIONAL

Review the reading, conversations, and picture drills for this lesson.

MULTIPLE-CHOICE

Choose the best sentence of the three in each group:

1. A) What are this?
   B) What is these?
   C) What are these?

2. A) They is cup.
   B) They is cups.
   C) They are cups.

3. A) This is a bowl.
   B) These is a bowl.
   C) Those is a bowl.

4. A) That is forks.
   B) That are forks.
   C) Those are forks.

5. Is this a plate?
   A) Yes, it is.
   B) Yes, she is.
   C) Yes, he is.

6. Are these knives?
   A) Yes, it are.
   B) Yes, we are.
   C) Yes, they are.

WRITING EXERCISE

1. Does the Baker house in Centerville have ten rooms?
2. What are the rooms?
3. Do the Bakers have a lot of things in their house?
4. What things do they have?

LESSON 4

MULTIPLE-CHOICE
Choose the best sentence of the three in each group.

1. A) He is a man.
   B) She is a man.
   C) They is a man.

2. A) They is boy.
   B) They is boys.
   C) They are boys.

3. A) Joan and Carol is girl.
   B) Joan and Carol are girl.
   C) Joan and Carol are girls.

4. A) Is Mrs. Baker woman?
   B) Is a woman Mrs. Baker?
   C) Is Mrs. Baker a woman?

5. Is Joan a girl?
   A) Yes, he is.
   B) Yes, she is.
   C) Yes, it is.

6. Are Peter and Tom boys?
   A) Yes, they boys.
   B) Yes, they are.
   C) Yes, they is.

WRITING EXERCISE
1. Are there three people in the Baker family?
2. Who are the girls?
3. Who are the boys?
4. Are there three people in your family?
5. Who are the girls?
6. Who are the boys?

LESSON 5

MULTIPLE-CHOICE
Choose the best sentence of the three in each group.

1. A) Joan is a secretary.
   B) Joan is secretary.
   C) Joan a secretary is.

2. A) Peter, Tom, and Carol is a student.
   B) Peter, Tom, and Carol are a student.
   C) Peter, Tom, and Carol are students.

3. A) Where Mr. Baker is?
   B) Is where Mr. Baker?
   C) Where is Mr. Baker?

4. Where is Tom?
   A) He is in the music room.
   B) He is on the music room.
   C) He is at the music room.

5. A) What Peter is doing?
   B) What doing is Peter?
   C) What is Peter doing?

6. A) He is studying Spanish.
   B) He studying Spanish.
   C) He is study Spanish.

WRITING EXERCISE

1. Is everybody in the Baker family busy?
2. What is Mr. Baker doing?
3. What is Mrs. Baker doing?
4. What is Peter doing?
5. What is Tom doing?
6. What is Carol doing?
7. What is Joan doing?

LESSON 6

OPTIONAL

Review the reading, conversations, and picture drills for this lesson.

MULTIPLE-CHOICE

Choose the best sentence of the three in each group.

1. A) Jerry is a boy.
   B) Jerry is boy.
   C) Jerry is boys.

2. A) Mr. Smith and Mr. Kent are man.
   B) Mr. Smith and Mr. Kent are mans.
   C) Mr. Smith and Mr. Kent are men.

3. A) Mary is a girl big.
   B) Mary is a big girl.
   C) Mary is big a girl.

4. A) Mrs. Clark is cooking now.
   B) Mrs. Clark is cook now.
   C) Mrs. Clark cooking now.

5. Which boy is singing?
   A) The tall boy is singing.
   B) The boy tall is singing.
   C) The tall is boy singing.

6. Which man is working?
   A) The man poor is working.
   B) The poor man is working.
   C) The poor is man working.

WRITING EXERCISE

1. Are Mr. Smith and Mr. Kent rich men?
2. Are Mrs. Clark and Mrs. Hill young women?
3. Are Jerry and Don tall boys?
4. Are Mary and Sharon small girls?

LESSON 7

OPTIONAL

Review the reading, conversations, and picture drills for this lesson.

MULTIPLE-CHOICE

Choose the best sentence of the three in each group.

1. A) How old is Jerry?
   B) How old Jerry is?
   C) How Jerry is old?

2. A) Mr. Hill is 41 years old.
   B) Mr. Hill has 41 years old.
   C) Mr. Hill is old 41 years.

3. A) Mrs. Hill is clean the house now.
   B) Mrs. Hill cleaning the house now.
   C) Mrs. Hill is cleaning the house now.

4. A) What Jerry's father doing now?
   B) What Jerry's father is doing now?
   C) What is Jerry's father doing now?

5. A) Linda's brother is swimming on the pool.
   B) Linda's brother is swimming in the pool.
   C) Linda's brother is swimming under the pool.

6. Is Jerry's mother cleaning now?
   A) Yes, she is.
   B) Yes, she cleaning.
   C) Yes, she's.

WRITING EXERCISE

1. Who is Jerry's father?
2. Who is Jerry's mother?
3. Does Jerry have a brother?
4. Does Jerry have a sister?
5. What is her name?
6. How old is she?

LESSON 8

OPTIONAL

Review the reading, conversations, and picture drills for this lesson.

MULTIPLE-CHOICE

Choose the best sentence of the three in each group.

1. A) Peter is 17 years old.
   B) Peter has 17 years old.
   C) Peter does 17 years old.

2. A) Jerry have black hair.
   B) Jerry has black hair.
   C) Jerry is black hair.

3. A) Tom and Carol have brown hair.
   B) Tom and Carol has brown hair.
   C) Tom and Carol is brown hair.

4. A) Linda's hair is black.
   B) Linda is hair black.
   C) Linda's is hair black.

5. A) She's eyes are brown.
   B) Her eyes are brown.
   C) Hers eyes are brown.

6. What color is Joan's hair?
   A) His hair is blond.
   B) Their hair is blond.
   C) Her hair is blond.

WRITING EXERCISE

1. How many families do we know in Centerville now?
2. Who are the people in the Baker family?
3. Who are the people in the Hill family?
4. Who are the other people in the Hill family?

LESSON 9

OPTIONAL

Review the reading, conversations, and picture drills for this lesson.

MULTIPLE-CHOICE

Choose the best sentence of the three in each group.

1. A) This bread is white.
    B) This bread are white.
    C) This bread does white.

2. A) Mrs. Baker doesn't have a butter.
    B) Mrs. Baker doesn't have any butter.
    C) Mrs. Baker doesn't have some butter.

3. A) She needs a eggs.
    B) She needs any eggs.
    C) She needs some eggs.

4. A) Does Mr. Baker have some flour?
    B) Does Mr. Baker has some flour?
    C) Does Mr. Baker had some flour?

5. Does Mrs. Baker have any meat?
    A) No, she haven't.
    B) No, she any.
    C) No, she doesn't.

6. Does she need some bananas?
    A) Yes, she need.
    B) Yes, she some.
    C) Yes, she does.

WRITING EXERCISE

1. Where does Mrs. Baker usually go every Saturday morning?
2. Who usually goes with her?
3. What does he do for her?
4. How does Mrs. Baker know what she needs to buy in the supermarket?

LESSON 10

OPTIONAL

Review the reading, conversations, and picture drills for this lesson.

MULTIPLE-CHOICE

1. A) Peter is get up.
    B) Peter gets up.
    C) Peter get up.

2. A) He is eat breakfast every morning.
    B) He eats breakfast every morning.
    C) He eat breakfast every morning.

3. A) He goes to school at eight thirty.
   B) He goes to school to eight thirty.
   C) He goes to school in eight thirty.

4. A) What time Peter goes home?
   B) What time Peter does go home?
   C) What time does Peter go home?

5. A) Does Peter listens to music every afternoon?
   B) Does Peter listen to music every afternoon?
   C) Listens Peter to music every afternoon?

6. Peter goes to bed at ten thirty, doesn't he?
   A) Yes, he goes.
   B) Yes, he is.
   C) Yes, he does.

WRITING EXERCISE

1. When does Peter usually get up?
2. When does Peter usually go to bed?
3. When do you usually get up?
4. What time do you usually go to bed?

LESSON 11

OPTIONAL

Review the reading, conversations, and picture drills for this lesson.

MULTIPLE-CHOICE

1. A) Does Mr. Anderson have many strength?
   B) Does Mr. Anderson have much strength?
   C) Does Mr. Anderson have few strength?

2. A) He has lot children.
   B) He has a lot children.
   C) He has a lot of children.

3. A) He doesn't have many books.
   B) He doesn't have lot books.
   C) He doesn't have much books.

4. A) Does he have much land?
   B) Is he have much land?
   C) Do he have much land?

5. Does he have many children?
   A) Yes, he have.
   B) Yes, he does.
   C) Yes, he much.

6. Does he have much money?
   A) No, he haven't.
   B) No, he doesn't.
   C) No, he not.

WRITING EXERCISE

1. What is the name of Mrs. Baker's brother?
2. What does he do?
3. Where does he live?
4. What does he have a lot of?
5. Does he have a lot of the things that many people in the city have?

LESSON 12

OPTIONAL

Review the reading, conversations, and picture drills for this lesson.

MULTIPLE-CHOICE

1. A) She is going to buy soft drinks tomorrow.
   B) She is going buy soft drinks tomorrow.
   C) She is going buys soft drinks tomorrow.

2. A) Linda is going to buy many candy tomorrow.
   B) Linda is going to buy a lot of candy tomorrow.
   C) Linda is going to buy much candy tomorrow.

3. A) Carol is going to buy a little cookies tomorrow.
   B) Carol is going to buy a small cookies tomorrow.
   C) Carol is going to buy a few cookies tomorrow.

4. A) She is going to buy a few soft drinks.
   B) She is going to buy a little soft drinks.
   C) She is going to buy a small soft drinks.

5. A) Is she going to buy a lot of fruit?
   B) Is going she to buy a lot of fruit?
   C) Is going to she buy a lot of fruit?

6. Is Carol going to buy a little cake?
   A) Yes, she going.
   B) Yes, she is.
   C) Yes, she buy.

WRITING EXERCISE

1. Who is Carol Baker?
2. How old is she?
3. When is she going to have a party?
4. Is she going to have a large party?
5. What is she going to buy for the party?

LESSON 13

OPTIONAL

Review the reading, conversations, and picture drills for this lesson.

MULTIPLE-CHOICE

1. A) Peter is going study engineering.
   B) Peter is going to study engineering.
   C) Peter is going to studies engineering.

2. A) Peter is going to be engineer.
   B) Peter is going to be a engineer.
   C) Peter is going to be an engineer.

3. A) Jerry is going to study law.
   B) Jerry is going to study lawing.
   C) Jerry is going to study lawyer.

4. A) Tom is going to be a music.
   B) Tom is going to be a musician.
   C) Tom is going to be a musicer.

5. A) What is going Carol to study?
   B) What Carol is going to study?
   C) What is Carol going to study?

6. Why is Linda going to studying nursing?
   A) Because she is going to be a nurse.
   B) Because she is going to do a nurse.
   C) Because she is going to study a nurse.

WRITING EXERCISE

1. Who is Sharon Carter?
2. What does her mother do?
3. How old is Sharon?
4. Does she have plans for the future?
5. What does she say she is going to study?
6. What does she say she is going to be?

LESSON 14

OPTIONAL

Review the reading, conversations, and picture drills for this lesson.

MULTIPLE-CHOICE

1. A) Is you know Tom?
   B) Does you know Tom?
   C) Do you know Tom?

2. A) I know he.
   B) I know him.
   C) I know his.

3. A) She is going to make a sweater for him.
   B) She is going to make a sweater to him.
   C) She is going to make a sweater at him.

4. A) Tom is going to play the guitar for they.
   B) Tom is going to play the guitar for their.
   C) Tom is going to play the guitar for them.

5. A) Carol is going to paint a picture for he.
   B) Carol is going to paint a picture for his.
   C) Carol is going to paint a picture for him.

6. Is Joan going to lend some money to Tom?
   A) Yes, she is.
   B) Yes, she lend.
   C) Yes, she going.

WRITING EXERCISE

1. How old will Mr. Baker be next Friday?
2. What is Mrs. Baker going to give him for his birthday?
3. What is Joan going to give him?
4. What is Peter going to give him?
5. What is Tom going to give him?
6. Are Mr. Baker's friends going to give him presents too?

LESSON 15

OPTIONAL

Review the reading, conversations, and picture drills for this lesson.

MULTIPLE-CHOICE

1. A) Jerry dressed before breakfast yesterday.
   B) Jerry is dressed before breakfast yesterday.
   C) Jerry dress before breakfast yesterday.

2. A) He walked to school.
   B) He is walked to school.
   C) He walk to school.

3. A) Did he played football in his gym class?
   B) Did he play football in his gym class?
   C) Played he football in his gym class?

4. A) When did he dress yesterday?
   B) When he did dress yesterday?
   C) When he dressed yesterday?

5. Did he walk downtown after school?
   A) No, he not.
   B) No, he isn't.
   C) No, he didn't.

6. Did he watch television after dinner?
   A) Yes, he watch.
   B) Yes, he did.
   C) Yes, he does.

WRITING EXERCISE

1. How did Jerry go to school yesterday?
2. What did Jerry do in his morning classes yesterday?
3. What did Jerry do in his afternoon classes yesterday?
4. What did Jerry do at home before dinner?
5. What did Jerry do at home after dinner?

LESSON 16

OPTIONAL

Review the reading, conversations, and picture drills for this lesson.

MULTIPLE-CHOICE

1. A) Linda got up at eight o'clock yesterday.
   B) Linda get up at eight o'clock yesterday.
   C) Linda getted up at eight o'clock yesterday.

2. A) She eat breakfast at eight thirty yesterday.
   B) She eated breakfast at eight thirty yesterday.
   C) She ate breakfast at eight thirty yesterday.

3. A) Did he gave her thirty dollars?
   B) Did he give her thirty dollars?
   C) Is he gave her thirty dollars?

4. A) She bought a blue dress, isn't it?
   B) She bought a blue dress, wasn't it?
   C) She bought a blue dress, didn't she?

5. Did she ride downtown on the bus yesterday?
   A) Yes, she is.
   B) Yes, she does.
   C) Yes, she did.

6. Didn't she go to a bookstore?
   A) No, she not go.
   B) No, she isn't.
   C) No, she didn't.

WRITING EXERCISE

1. Where did Linda go yesterday?
2. What did Linda buy yesterday?
3. Where did Linda eat lunch?
4. How did Linda come home?

LESSON 17

MULTIPLE-CHOICE

1. A) Carol is at the library last night.
   B) Carol was at the library last night.
   C) Carol were at the library last night

2. A) Mr. and Mrs. Baker were at a friend's house last night.
   B) Mr. and Mrs. Baker are at a friend's house last night.
   C) Mr. and Mrs. Baker was at a friend's house last night.

3. A) Tom was play basketball.
   B) Tom was played basketball.
   C) Tom was playing basketball.

4. A) Peter and Joan were see a movie.
   B) Peter and Joan were saw a movie.
   C) Peter and Joan were seeing a movie.

5. A) They weren't at home, weren't they?
   B) They weren't at home, were they?
   C) They weren't at home, did they?

6. Were Mr. and Mrs. Baker at a friend's house last night?
   A) Yes, they are.
   B) Yes, they at.
   C) Yes, they were.

WRITING EXERCISE

1. Where were Peter's father and mother last night?
2. What were they doing?
3. Where was Carol last night.
4. What was she doing?
5. Where was Tom last night?
6. What was he doing?
7. Where were Peter and Joan?
8. What were they doing?
9. Was anybody home last night?

Grammar Index

Grammar Index

A

F

G

H

I

K

L

M

N

O

P

Q

S

W

Y